Fodor's InFocus

ZION AND BRYCE CANYON NATIONAL PARKS

T0063746

Welcome to Zion and Bryce Canyon National Parks

Zion and Bryce Canyon are well known for their hoodoos, slot canyons, and other red-rock formations. But different landscapes also await, from hanging gardens to emerald pools. There's plenty of history, too—ruins, petroglyphs, pioneer graffiti, and ghost towns memorialize what once was. As you plan your trip to Zion and Bryce Canyon National Parks, please confirm that places are still open and let us know when we need to make updates by writing to us at editors@fodors.com.

TOP REASONS TO GO

★ **Hiking:** Trails meander beside rivers, through woods, along or under canyon rims, and amid hoodoos.

★ **Family Fun:** Park programs and outdoor adventures make family vacations a pleasure.

★ **Scenic Drives:** Routes traverse scenery that takes in snowcapped mountains as well as colorful desert.

★ **Stargazing:** Clear skies make astronomy a highlight throughout the region.

★ **R&R Aplenty:** Careen down a mountain; hit the greens; unwind in a spa; dine with a view.

Contents

Chapter 1

EXPERIENCE ZION AND BRYCE CANYON NATIONAL PARKS

15 ULTIMATE EXPERIENCES

Zion and Bryce Canyon National Parks offer terrific experiences that should be on every traveler's list. Here are Fodor's top picks for a memorable trip.

1 Exploring canyons

Hike through narrow slot canyons on trails or in water, rappel down from above, or climb canyon walls in the two national parks and nearby areas. *(Ch. 3, 4, 5, 6)*

2 Hiking along a river

Strap on sturdy water shoes, and bring a walking stick and sense of adventure to hike up the Virgin River between the towering canyon walls of The Narrows. *(Ch. 3)*

3 Exploring on horseback

Even beginners and kids can saddle up for a guided horseback ride in either Zion or Bryce; a trek in the latter allows for an up-close look at the amphitheater. *(Ch. 3, 5)*

4 Wandering amid hanging gardens

Zion's "hanging gardens" are a must-see—lush flowers and ferns hang down from the cliff rocks, their roots fed by water dripping down the walls. See them on the Riverside Walk and by the Emerald Pools. *(Ch. 3)*

5 Hitting the trail

Miles and miles of hiking, biking, and equestrian trails run through the national parks, forests, and nature preserves of southern Utah. Bring sturdy shoes! *(Ch. 3, 4, 5, 6)*

6 Bird-watching

With nearly 300 bird species identified between the two parks, birders will want to bring their binoculars to see which ones they can spot. Park websites have printable bird lists. *(Ch. 3, 5)*

7 Visiting Snow Canyon

Experience a natural desert habitat near St. George at Snow Canyon State Park, where wildlife is abundant and trails lead to lava cones, petrified dunes, and cactus gardens. *(Ch. 4)*

8 Gazing at the night sky

Both parks are outstanding for stargazing. Bryce has night-sky ranger programs and a summer astronomy festival. Photograph the Milky Way at Kodachrome Basin State Park. *(Ch. 3, 5, 6)*

9 Experiencing hoodoo heaven

Bryce Canyon's thin, tall rock spires called "hoodoos" range from human height to 10 stories tall. You can also find them in Red Canyon and Cedar Breaks National Monument, both nearby. *(Ch. 5, 6)*

10 Seeing sand pipes

At Kodachrome Basin State Park, you can see 67 "sand pipes"— stone spires found nowhere else on Earth. Be sure to bring your camera to this park named after the color film. *(Ch. 6)*

11 Biking through the parks

Skip the shuttle lines on an invigorating bike ride along the main drives in either Zion or Bryce Canyon (or both!). You can catch a shuttle back if you'd prefer. *(Ch. 3, 5)*

12 Driving Highway 12 Scenic Byway

The journey really is the destination on this epic, 123-mile route, an "All-American Road" that starts near Bryce Canyon and travels northeast. *(Ch. 5, 6)*

13 Exploring Hole-in-the-Rock Road

Retrace a pioneer route on this 60-mile dirt road through Grand Staircase–Escalante National Monument. *(Ch. 6)*

14 Peering down from on high

The steep hike up to Angels Landing rewards with jaw-dropping views down into Zion Canyon. At the very least, be sure to peek down into Bryce Canyon, which you can do safely from the rim. *(Ch. 3, 5)*

15 Adventuring in the backcountry

Intrepid adventurers can explore unique geological features like The Subway at Zion and escape from the crowds overnight at primitive campgrounds in both parks. *(Ch. 3, 5)*

WHAT'S WHERE

1 Zion National Park. Utah's most visited park can get quite crowded during the spring–fall peak season, but it's still a thrilling place, with starry skies, soaring canyons, and fascinating natural wonders.

2 Zion National Park Gateways. Springdale adjoins the park and offers a free shuttle service and plenty of lodging and dining options. Tiny Hurricane is 22 miles west; 18 miles farther is the sizable city of St. George. Orderville is 18 miles east of Zion en route to Bryce Canyon. Kanab—which offers plenty of travel services—is about 30 miles southeast of Zion's East Entrance.

3 Bryce Canyon National Park. The smaller of the two parks can be experienced in a day, but longer stays allow for a more leisurely and thorough exploration of Bryce Canyon's unique landscape, even beyond its iconic hoodoos. It's 84 miles from Zion via Highway 9, U.S. 89, and Highway 12.

4 Bryce Canyon National Park Gateways. Panguitch, 24 miles northwest of Bryce Canyon, is also a good base for visiting Cedar Breaks National Monument, which is close to the ski town of Brian Head and the college town of Cedar City. Tiny Bryce Canyon City and Tropic are just outside the park. Escalante, a recreation hub, is 48 miles northeast via Scenic Byway 12.

Birds, Reptiles, and Mammals of Zion and Bryce Canyon

PEREGRINE FALCON
With wingspans of more than 3 feet, these falcons are often spotted near their nesting sites along cliffs and rocky ledges. Look for them in quieter, southern portions of Bryce Canyon as well as the Fairyland Point area.

GREAT BASIN RATTLESNAKE
One of the parks' most famous and feared inhabitants waits for its prey to approach. These snakes have excellent eyesight, so stay on trails to avoid an unexpected encounter, and seek immediate medical attention if bitten.

UTAH PRAIRIE DOG
They might look cuddly, but keep your distance. Some people make the mistake of feeding them, but doing so contributes to the rodent's lack of fear of humans. They carry diseases that could be lethal if they bite you.

BIGHORN SHEEP
Look for the rams (male) and ewes (female) in the Checkerboard Mesa area of Zion. The hollow-horned animals are especially active in fall. With padded hooves, they are uniquely suited to the steep, rocky slopes and canyons.

CLARK'S NUTCRACKER
Found throughout Bryce Canyon, these gray-and-black birds feed on the nuts from pine trees and also store tens of thousands of nuts in the ground, which facilitates the sprouting of new trees.

Gray fox

WATER OUZEL
Commonly known as the American dipper, this aquatic songbird is seen and heard by Zion's rivers. It stands alongside shallow waters, constantly dipping its head in to find food.

WILD TURKEY
At dusk in Zion National Park, look up and you may spy a flock of turkeys, which appear as silhouettes in the trees. Look for their colorful heads and dark bodies, which may have white tips on rich plumage.

WHIPTAIL LIZARD
Named for the way their tails swish side to side while running, these lizards are common to Zion. You can spot them in desert scrub, grasslands, and pine forests.

GRAY FOX
Not uncommon but hard to spot, these foxes are mainly nocturnal. They have unique hooked claws and a rotating forearm that allows them to climb trees. They eat small mammals, insects, fruit, and nuts.

PRONGHORN
With a spring that appears almost effortless as they bound across the meadows of the high plateau of Bryce Canyon, the pronghorns are beautiful sights to behold. While they are a frequent sight in the meadows at Bryce Canyon from spring through fall, Pronghorn retreat to lower elevations, where there is less snow, in the winter.

Plants of Zion and Bryce Canyon

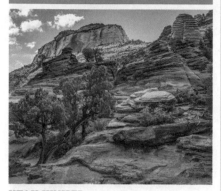

UTAH JUNIPER

Seen below the rim at Bryce Canyon and in the pygmy woodland of Zion, these short trees have edible blue berries that are used for medicinal purposes, for making beads, and for giving gin its unique flavor.

BIG SAGEBRUSH

This shrub grows in thick patches along trails in Zion. Rub the silvery, blue-green leaves to experience a fragrance described by one writer as "camphor blended with a touch of Christmas." Native Americans burn it to use the smoke for purification.

BRISTLECONE PINE

Bryce Canyon (at Yovimpa Point) is home to a pine that is more than 1,600 years old. The species' highly resinous wood and needles that don't fall off for 40 years help extend its longevity (the trees are among the oldest living organisms on Earth).

BRYCE CANYON PAINTBRUSH

This rare species of the figwort family grows—no taller than 6 inches—only in the park (hence its name). The delicate fuchsia flower blooms from May through August.

FREMONT COTTONWOOD

The presence of these trees indicates a long-term water source. Look for them along the Virgin River in Zion National Park. Younger trees have smooth bark; older ones develop deeply furrowed, whitish, cracked bark.

MAIDENHAIR FERN

One of 20 fern species in Zion, the delicate-leaved, moisture-loving plants can be seen in the hanging gardens that grow along the sides of cliffs and near the Emerald Pools. Ferns reproduce via spores rather than seeds.

PINYON PINE

Found at Bryce Canyon, these slow-growing trees with crooked trunks have massive root systems. Their nutritious, valuable pine nuts drop in the fall. You're welcome to snack on them, but resist the temptation to harvest enough for a batch of pesto.

Fremont cottonwood

PONDEROSA PINE

You can easily identify these trees by their tall, straight trunks and reddish-orange, puzzle-piece-shaped bark that smells like vanilla. Named for their heavy "ponderous" wood, these pines are found throughout both national parks.

QUAKING ASPEN

Look for these trees on level, moist ground as well as on dry slopes. Their bark is smooth, and their leaves, which turn a brilliant golden hue each autumn, seem to quiver in the breeze—hence, their name.

ROCK COLUMBINE

The blue of these flowers contrasts with the red cliffs and soil of Bryce Canyon, making them one of the park's more distinctive plants. Highly regarded for their beauty, they've been used for ornamentation and perfumes for centuries.

Best Trails of Zion and Bryce Canyon

RIM TRAIL
A lovely stroll along the Bryce Amphitheater rim between Sunset and Sunrise Points, this 1-mile trail is accessible to wheelchairs and strollers. Pets on leashes are welcome. Bring your camera in the evening for sunset photos of glowing hoodoos.

NAVAJO LOOP
This steep but short route descends to Bryce's amphitheater via switchbacks and a narrow hallway of rock called Wall Street. Another trail back makes it an hour round-trip.

RIVERSIDE WALK
On this easy Zion stroll along the river, see wildflowers, hanging gardens, and The Narrows. Strollers can roll through without trouble; wheelchairs may need assistance. Round-trip, the 2.2-mile walk takes about 90 minutes.

QUEEN'S GARDEN TRAIL
The "essential Bryce sampler" trail descends 350 feet to the amphitheater, then to a tunnel and a ground-level view of the hoodoos. Although it gets crowded, it's a great route for families.

ANGELS LANDING TRAIL
One of Zion's most challenging hikes has switchbacks and a narrow path with chain handrails. It's not for kids or the height-averse, and you must obtain a permit to climb it, but the 360-degree, top-side views are astounding.

PA'RUS TRAIL

Zion's only trail open to bikes and leashed pets is flat, paved, and easy. You'll catch views of The Watchman, The Temples, and Towers of the Virgin. Plus, you can dip your toes in the Virgin River.

THE NARROWS

Zion Canyon's narrowest section (20–30 feet wide) has 1,000-foot walls. Hikers wade through the Virgin River, following the trail up on a short or long trek; hiking from the top down requires rappelling and a permit.

PEEKABOO LOOP

A steep, strenuous Bryce Canyon trail leads to The Wall of Windows and the Three Wise Men. Note that horses share the route and have the right-of-way. Allow three to four hours to hike the 5-mile trail.

EMERALD POOLS TRAIL

This relatively easy path starts across from Zion Lodge and passes waterfalls en route to the lower pool. It's all most impressive in spring when the snow melts; fall visits may be less vibrant.

CANYON OVERLOOK TRAIL

From the east entrance of Zion, this popular, 1-mile, round-trip trail takes about an hour. It's moderately steep, with a 180-foot elevation gain to reach the overlook and the breathtaking views. Come early for a parking spot; it's not reachable by shuttle bus.

Welcome to Zion and Bryce Canyon

Look up, look down, repeat—as many times as necessary. Bryce Canyon and Zion are truly "vertical" experiences, with chasms and towers galore. Standing at the base of 2,000 feet of sheer rock in Zion's Virgin River Canyon, feel the cool canyon breezes. Even on summer's hottest days, cottonwoods rustle, and dozens of birds and mammals congregate in this "place of sanctuary" from the searing desert heat.

GEOLOGICAL HISTORY

Zion and Bryce offer an up-close look at millions of years of geological history. With the exception of nearby Cedar Breaks National Monument, you'll be hard-pressed to find hoodoos like Bryce's anywhere on the planet. Two key steps in a giant staircase, these brilliant places are just a small section of a massive Southwest puzzle, where geologists are still unlocking the secrets to earth's history from the predinosaur eras to the present.

The Grand Staircase spans more than 150 miles, from the Paunsaugunt Plateau of Bryce Canyon (Yovimpa Point is 9,100 feet above sea level) to the Grand Canyon's south rim (6,800 feet). Deep canyons slice through, creating some places that are only nominally above sea level.

Bryce sits on top as the youngest sibling. A series of amphitheaters, its oldest layers are a mere 65 million years old. Erosion and frost-wedging (frequent freezing and thawing of moisture in rock) has shaped the multihued rock into the canyons, arches, and spires of today.

Zion Canyon is one of the middle siblings; its oldest layers date back 240 million years. Zion was once a flat basin near sea level, but erosion from nearby mountains resulted in both its deep, slender gorges and its wide canyons.

PEOPLE OF THE LANDS

Evidence of human settlements in the lush, cool delta of Zion's Virgin River dates from as early as AD 500, when the Virgin Anasazi (Ancestral Puebloan) and Parowan Fremont created year-round agricultural communities. Here, bow-and-arrow use became widespread. Both civilizations disappear from archaeological records about AD 1300, apparently victims of droughts and intermittent catastrophic flooding. The Southern Paiute appear to have filled the void for some of the ensuing 500 years, before Euro-American explorations began to crisscross the Southwest on the Old Spanish Trail.

Brigham Young's Church of Jesus Christ of Latter-day Saints arrived in Utah in 1847, and by 1863, Isaac Behunin had built the first log cabin in Zion Canyon. Behunin, full of religious fervor, is credited with naming Zion. Mormon settlers added many of the religion-suffused names, such as The Three Patriarchs, The Great White Throne, Angels Landing, and at least three temples (East, West, and Sinawava).

Mormon settlers arrived in Bryce Canyon in the 1850s and 1860s, but their livestock grazing threatened the food sources of the Paiute tribe that hunted and gathered in the area. Wars ensued, many lives on both sides were lost, and most settlers left. Beginning in the early 1870s, the settlers returned and reestablished small farming communities, grazing their sheep and cows in the present-day park lands.

ESTABLISHING THE PARKS

In 1909, the area of present-day Zion was formally preserved as Mukuntuweap National Monument. After the government granted national park status to Zion in 1919, visitation grew through aggressive promotion, politicking, and development by the Union Pacific Railroad that slowly improved access to southern Utah—an important tourism destination on the railroad's western network. Construction of the Zion–Mt. Carmel Highway in 1930 shortened travel times throughout the Southwest and increased the park's popularity.

Bryce Canyon first began to move into America's consciousness in the years after the Civil War. Grove Karl Gilbert wrote of "a perfect wilderness … the stunningest thing out of a picture." His words, along with sketches by John E. Weyss and increased Mormon settlement across southern Utah, attracted the interest of writers, artists, and traders.

When J. W. Humphrey became a National Park Service (NPS) supervisor in 1915, extensive explorations of the area began—and rail barons took notice. Union Pacific officials saw Bryce as a key link for their growing Grand Canyon North Rim business, which had a longer tourism season than Yellowstone, their signature attraction at the time.

In 1927, Union Pacific and the NPS negotiated a historic swap. In exchange for more than 11 acres at Bryce Canyon, the park service agreed to build the Zion–Mt. Carmel tunnel. In 1928, Bryce Canyon was officially designated a national park. What resulted was the protection and preservation of what Bryce historian Nicholas Scrattish called "one of the world's best sites for an appreciation of the inexorable, titanic forces which have shaped the globe's surface."

A VAST REGION OF WONDERS

Zion and Bryce Canyon national parks are dual centerpieces of a massive wilderness stretching from Arizona's Grand Canyon north to Interstate 70, which crosses the center of eastern Utah. The two parks are among the most recognized natural wonders in the Western United States as well as a microcosm of the region's geological and topographical diversity.

This is a land of adventure and contemplation, of adrenaline and retreat. It's not an either-or proposition: you can rejuvenate just as well while soaking at a luxury spa as you can by scampering up to the rim of a rugged canyon. Ruins, petroglyphs, pioneer graffiti, and ghost towns—monuments to what once was—beckon new explorers.

The region's secrets reveal themselves to seekers, yet some mysteries remain elusive—the paradox of a bustling world hidden by the impression of silent, open space. Such contrasts have always attracted the curious. Famed explorer John Wesley Powell charted the uncharted; the young idealist and dreamer Everett Ruess left his wealthy family and was lost without a trace in the canyons; the late author and curmudgeon Edward Abbey found himself.

But that's the beauty of this place, the joy of choice in a land that confronts and challenges. We come, ostensibly, to escape; yet we really come to discover.

What to Watch and Read

BETWEEN A ROCK AND A HARD PLACE

In 2003, while exploring southeastern Utah's canyons, Aron Ralston became trapped in a narrow crevasse. For five days, he struggled to break free from the 800-pound boulder that had crushed his arm, reflecting on his life as he faced his mortality. He eventually amputated his arm, rappelled to the canyon floor, and hiked out. His story was dramatized on the big screen in *127 Hours,* starring James Franco.

BUTCH CASSIDY AND THE SUNDANCE KID

Paul Newman and Robert Redford starred in this classic 1969 western about Utah's most infamous outlaws. Katharine Ross played Etta, Sundance's lover. Many of the scenes were shot in and around Zion National Park and in the nearby ghost town of Grafton.

CANYON WILDERNESS OF THE SOUTHWEST

Photographer Jon Ortner visited more than 50 locations in the canyon lands of Utah and Arizona, including 10 national parks, to shoot the more than 200 spectacularly scenic photos in this book.

DEATH IN ZION NATIONAL PARK: STORIES OF ACCIDENTS AND FOOLHARDINESS IN UTAH'S GRAND CIRCLE

Author Randi Minetor says that Zion is her favorite national park of the hundreds of sites she and her husband have visited. In this book, she recounts the stories of those whose own visits to Zion resulted in fatalities. From falls off cliffs to the tragic loss of seven hikers in 2015 from a flash flood, the dangers of unpredictable weather, missteps on trails, being unprepared for hazards, and more are detailed. You may find yourself reviewing safety considerations quite carefully before heading out on trails after reading this.

DESERT SOLITAIRE

Edward Abbey wrote many books—both fiction and nonfiction—about the desert Southwest, and this, published in 1968, is considered one of his best. It recounts his experiences during three seasons as a national park ranger.

IN SEARCH OF THE OLD ONES: EXPLORING THE ANASAZI WORLD OF THE SOUTHWEST

In this book, climber and mountaineer David Roberts takes readers on an archaeological expedition as he uncovers and explores Ancestral Puebloan sites and shares insights about their culture.

RED: PASSION AND PATIENCE IN THE DESERT

Prolific writer and naturalist Terry Tempest Williams shares an intimate look at the desert canyon lands of southern Utah, where she has lived all her life. Her personal stories are entwined with historical accounts, giving a rich sense of place to the red-rock lands.

STANDING ON THE WALLS OF TIME: ANCIENT ART OF UTAH'S CLIFFS AND CANYONS

Author Kevin T. Jones, an archaeologist, teamed up with rock-art researcher and photographer Layne Miller to create this fascinating book that showcases an array of rock art throughout the region.

ZION CANYON: TREASURE OF THE GODS

This 37-minute documentary was originally filmed for IMAX. In addition to outstanding views from above area canyons, the film includes dramatized vignettes of Zion's history and legends, as well as some intense hold-your-breath climbing scenes. Though it was released in 1996, the large-format cinematography translates well to today's large-screen TVs and surround sound (or skip the sound if you find that the music and acting detract from the scenic majesty). Lean back in a comfy chair with some popcorn, and enjoy the immersive experience.

Chapter 2

TRAVEL SMART

Updated by
Andrew Collins

♟ STATE POPULATION:
3.4 million

LANGUAGE:
Englich

$ CURRENCY:
U.S. dollar

☎ AREA CODE:
435

⚠ EMERGENCIES:
911

🚗 DRIVING:
On the right

⚡ ELECTRICITY:
120–220 v/60 cycles; plugs have two or three rectangular prongs

🕙 TIME:
Mountain Time, 2 hours behind New York

🌐 WEB RESOURCES:
www.nps.gov/brca, www.nps.gov/zion, www.zionpark.com, www.vlsltutah.com

✈ AIRPORT:
Salt Lake City International Airport (SLC), St. George Regional Airport (SGU), Harry Reid International Airport (LAS)

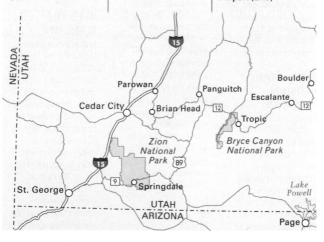

Know Before You Go

Several million people experience the wonders of Zion every year, and many venture on to see the hoodoos and heights of nearby Bryce Canyon. These tips will help you make the most of your visit while keeping the parks preserved for years to come.

ALWAYS WEAR SUNSCREEN

The sun shines long and hot here. In fact, Utah is one of the top 10 sunniest states (and has among the highest rates of skin cancer). Use sunscreen every day, even in winter. Wearing a wide-brimmed hat and sunglasses with ultraviolet protection is essential, too. At high altitudes, UV exposure increases; elevations in this region range from 3,000 to 10,000 feet.

UNDERSTAND ALTITUDE SICKNESS

Symptoms of altitude sickness include shortness of breath due to lack of oxygen, dizziness, nausea, and headaches. This unpleasant condition can start affecting people at elevations as low as 4,000 feet and become progressively more severe the higher you go. It's a common challenge for visitors to the entire area, but especially at Bryce Canyon National Park and Cedar Breaks National Monument, which exceed 8,000 feet in elevation. It's best to acclimate gradually, stay hydrated, reduce alcohol consumption, and rest—or even descend—if you experience any symptoms. Take at least a day to adjust to the thin mountain air before descending the Bryce Canyon Amphitheater since the only way out is back up the steep trail.

BE A SMART EXPLORER

There are endless ways to explore the outdoors—hiking, biking, climbing, horseback riding, rafting—but there are risks, too. The National Park Service recommends eating well, drinking at least a gallon of water a day, packing all recommended supplies, avoiding strenuous activities at midday, and wearing sturdy shoes. It's best not to head out alone, but if you do, let someone know where you're going and when you plan to return. If you get lost, always wait where you are for rescue. Make sure you have all necessary permits for backcountry and overnight trips, too.

HEED THE ELEMENTS

Hazardous conditions (fallen trees, rock slides, flash floods) can suddenly and temporarily close roads, trails, and other areas of the parks at any time—though rangers try their best to keep delays short. Park and town visitor centers have the most recent information about closures, as well as the latest weather forecasts, which are important to know before heading out for a long hike or remote drive, especially in summer, when thunderstorms are a constant threat. Be prepared for sudden weather changes, and stay low if there's lightning. In winter, make sure your vehicle is prepared for cold-weather driving conditions, including sudden and heavy snowfall.

KEEP YOUR DISTANCE

Although you're unlikely to encounter dangerous animals, even if a creature seems tame or cute and cuddly, rely on your camera or binoculars to get a closer view. Never feed wild animals—even birds and small mammals (for their safety as much as for your own)—and if you see one that's sick or injured, contact a park ranger rather than approaching it.

LEAVE NO TRACE

Within the national parks, it's illegal to pick wildflowers, take specimens, or otherwise disturb plants, rocks, or trees. Adopt a "leave-no-trace" policy: when you leave an area, take anything you brought with you and nothing more. Likewise, follow signs for closures and other regulations. These are in place for your safety and for the preservation of the wild and beautiful terrain.

CONSIDER YOUR PET

It might be best to board your pet at a private kennel in one of the gateway towns. As at most national parks, Zion and Bryce Canyon forbid pets in the backcountry, on trails, at viewpoints, in buildings, and on shuttles. Although Zion's Pa'rus Trail near the park entrance welcomes leashed pets, you may want to think twice about bringing Fido here as the trail is also used by bicyclists, who may distract your animal. For dog-friendly trails, head to Red Canyon in the Dixie National Forest or one of the state parks.

KNOW THE LAWS

Utah has strict liquor laws, a result of the longstanding influence of the Mormon church, which forbids members from drinking alcohol. The maximum ABV limit for beer sold at grocery stores and bars is 5%; for anything stronger, you must go to a liquor store or a restaurant. Note, too, that most area bars don't stay open very late, and it's a bad idea to drink and drive: Utah has the nation's lowest allowable blood-alcohol level (.05%). In addition, marijuana is illegal except with a medical card.

PLAN AHEAD (BUT GO WITH THE FLOW)

For peak-season visits, reserve hotels or campsites well in advance, especially for in-park stays. Permits for exploring Zion's highly popular wilderness generally require a reservation weeks or months before arrival. That said, be open to spontaneous experiences. Leave room in your itinerary to follow a ranger's recommendation or allow the pioneer spirit to take you on an improvised adventure.

Getting Here and Around

Separated by about 90 miles (along picturesque U.S. 89), Zion and Bryce Canyon national parks attract millions of visitors annually. Plan on three to five hours of driving from the closest major airports (Las Vegas and Salt Lake City), but savor the time spent on some of the Southwest's most memorable scenic drives.

Weather and elevation are two important considerations here. In summer, flash floods and incendiary heat (well over 110°F at low elevations) can be real perils. In winter, many back roads at the higher elevations are impassable due to snow and/or extreme cold.

Travel by horseback, bicycle, ATV, 4X4, and other means can be thrilling adventures, but be aware that natural elements can be deadly for the unprepared traveler. ⚠ **Gas stations in this part of the country may be more than 100 miles apart—and many places in this heavily Mormon part of the state are closed on Sunday.**

✈ Air

Both Salt Lake City (a hub of Delta Airlines) and Las Vegas airports are big international hubs served by all major airlines.

AIRPORTS

The major gateway to Utah is Salt Lake City International Airport, but a more convenient gateway to southern Utah, particularly if you're going only to Zion, is Harry Reid International Airport in Las Vegas. Bryce Canyon is equidistant between the two airports. Booming St. George's small airport has daily flights to Salt Lake City (on Delta), Phoenix (on American), and Denver (on United), and Cedar City's tiny airport has daily flights on Delta to Salt Lake City.

🚌 Bus

Greyhound buses run to St. George, from which St. George Shuttle offers bus service to Zion National Park. In addition, National Park Express offers bus service directly to Zion from Las Vegas, about 3 hours away; these buses also run from Zion to Bryce Canyon National Park.

From March through November (and during the Christmas to New Year's holiday period), Zion Canyon Scenic Drive is closed to private vehicles (except for guests at Zion Lodge), and you must take the free park shuttle. A second free shuttle runs between Springdale and the park's South Entrance. Adventure companies, such as Zion Guru and Zion Rock and Mountain Guides, also offer scheduled and on-demand shuttle rides to trailheads in Zion.

At Bryce Canyon, a free park shuttle stops at most of the viewpoints and trailheads in the northern half of the park (including Bryce Amphitheater and Bryce Point). The road is also open to private vehicles, but using the shuttle can be handy in high season, when parking spots are sometimes tough to come by.

🚗 Car

Driving both to and through the parks is never dull, given the spectacular scenery. Before setting out, make sure your vehicle is in top condition. And in this remote region, you should make sure your vehicle is prepared for emergencies, with flares or reflector triangles, jumper cables, an empty gas can, a fire extinguisher, a flashlight, a plastic tarp, blankets, and water.

CAR RENTALS

The airports in Salt Lake City and Las Vegas are served by all the major car rental companies, and you can also rent from Budget at Cedar City Regional Airport and from several big agencies at St. George Regional Airport. An economy car generally runs around $40 daily and $200 weekly, but these rates can fluctuate wildly depending on demand; Harry Reid International Airport generally has cheaper rates than the Utah airports.

GASOLINE

In urban areas like St. George and Cedar City, gas prices run slightly higher than the U.S. national average. In more remote towns and close to the parks, gas typically costs 10 to 30 cents a gallon more, and gas prices in Nevada are about 30 to 50 cents higher than in Utah. Gas stations are plentiful through the St. George–Cedar City corridor, and most stay open late (some are open 24 hours). In rural towns, as well as along remote stretches of interstate, stations are less frequent and hours are more limited, particularly on Sunday, although many stations have automated pumps that run 24/7. ⚠ **On back roads in remote areas, it's possible to drive 100 miles without passing a gas station, so always top your tank before heading into the backcountry.**

PARKING

All the hotels around Zion and Bryce Canyon as well as the visitor centers have lots with free parking. That said, it can be tough to find parking spaces

Getting Here and Around

inside the parks during busy periods, so consider taking the park shuttle in Bryce (in Zion Canyon, much of the year, the shuttle is your only option).

ROAD CONDITIONS

Utah has some of the world's most spectacular vistas—and challenging driving. Routes range from multilane blacktop to narrow dirt roads, from twisting switchbacks bordered by guardrails to primitive tracks so narrow that you must back up to the edge of a steep cliff to make a turn. Scenic routes and lookout points are clearly marked, so you can readily take in the views. Highways and the national parks are crowded in summer but typically receive far less traffic (and are occasionally impassable, especially in and around Bryce) in winter.

Watch out for wildlife on the road, especially at dawn and dusk. In winter, expect snow and icy roads; it's best to have a four-wheel-drive vehicle or carry snow chains, especially in the Bryce Canyon area.

ROADSIDE EMERGENCIES

Call ☎ 911 for emergencies, such as an accident or a serious health concern. For automotive breakdowns, call a towing service or the Utah Highway Patrol.

RVS AND TRAILERS

Vehicles over 13'1" high, 40' long, or weighing more than 50,000 pounds are banned on the Zion–Mt. Carmel Highway (Highway 9) within Zion National Park, as are commercial trucks, vehicles towing a trailer with a combined length of 50 feet or more, and vehicles carrying hazardous materials. This eastern approach to Zion runs through a 90-year-old, mile-long tunnel that is too small for many contemporary RVs.

In addition, any vehicles greater than 7'10" wide or 11'4" high will require a $15 permit and assistance from rangers (who will close the tunnel to one-way traffic when you pass through it). Each fee is good for two trips through the tunnel during a seven-day period, and the schedule for oversize vehicles is daily 8 am to 7 pm from late March through early October (till 4:30 pm the rest of the year).

🚆 Train

Amtrak has service to Las Vegas, Salt Lake City, and St. George.

Essentials

 Accessibility

Although many structures and facilities in both parks date back to the early 20th century, both Bryce and Zion are pretty strong in terms of accessibility. The visitor centers, shuttle buses, and park lodges in the parks are all accessible, and each park has at least some wheelchair-friendly trails and overlooks as well as accessible campsites.

Admission Fees

The entrance fees for Zion National Park and Bryce Canyon National Park are identical (and good for seven days): $35 per vehicle, $30 for motorcycles, and $20 if entering on foot, by park shuttle bus, or by bicycle (kids 15 and under are free). For $70 you can buy an annual pass for Zion or Bryce Canyon National Park.

■ TIP→ If you plan to visit more than one park in a year, save money with an Interagency Annual Pass, which gets you into all national parks properties as well as all other federal recreation sites for just $80. ⊕ *store. usgs.gov/recreational-passes*

Dining

Restaurants in southwestern Utah tend toward informal and often specialize in classic American fare along with Mexican and Southwestern cooking; steaks, burgers, and short-order fried foods dominate menus at many older spots. Increasingly, farm-to-table and international dining has taken hold in the region, especially in St. George, Cedar City, Springdale, and Kanab. Most tourist-oriented restaurants have liquor licenses, but there are still quite a few eateries in Utah that don't serve any alcohol, and many close on Sunday, too.

ZION RESTAURANTS

There's just one full-service restaurant, the Red Rock Grill at Zion Lodge, inside the park. Next door, there's also a casual outdoor café with a beer garden cart. Bordering the park, however, the town of Springdale has quite a few dining options, an increasing number of them serving sophisticated, globally influenced cuisine. To the east, you'll find only a handful of options near the park in and around Orderville, but Kanab, to the south, has a burgeoning little dining scene.

Essentials

BRYCE CANYON RESTAURANTS

Inside the park, The Lodge at Bryce Canyon serves above-average American cuisine in a charming, historic space. There's also a casual pizza parlor and a general store serving food in the park. In the nearest town, Bryce Canyon City, a handful of eateries serve pretty mediocre food. You're better off driving a bit farther, to the small towns of Tropic and Panguitch, which offer a few quite good options. Still farther afield, Cedar City and Kanab offer a nice range of dining options, including some destination-worthy spots serving creative contemporary fare.

PAYING

Most restaurants take credit cards, but some smaller places may not. It's worth asking.

RESERVATIONS AND DRESS

Virtually every restaurant in the region is casual, and none expect dressy attire. Neither of the park lodge restaurants accepts reservations, and outside the parks, reservations—though almost never required—can be a good idea on weekends and in the high season.

MEALS AND MEALTIMES

Restaurants both in the parks and in nearby towns typically close early in the evening, between 8 and 9 or even before then; it's always a good idea to check before heading out. Establishments that serve breakfast often open quite early—by 6 or 7 in the morning—especially near the parks.

WINE, BEER, AND SPIRITS

Despite what you may have heard, it's not hard to get a drink in Utah (assuming you're 21 or older). Many restaurants serve wine and beer—and occasionally liquor. Others are BYOB but may charge a corkage fee. Beer with 5% alcohol by volume is available in grocery and some convenience stores. For anything else, you'll have to go to a state liquor store—you'll find these in most of the major towns in the region, including Springdale, Kanab, Panguitch, Cedar City, and St. George; they're closed on Sunday. Note that the maximum legal blood-alcohol level permitted in drivers in Utah is 0.05%.

SMOKING

Smoking is banned in all restaurants and bars.

What It Costs			
$	$$	$$$	$$$$
AT DINNER			
under $20	$20–$30	$31–$40	over $40

✚ Health and Safety

For summer backcountry hikes, rangers warn about heat stroke, dehydration, disorientation, flash floods, cougars, bears, lightning, rattlesnakes, and a few other hazards. In winter, hypothermia and blizzards are the biggest dangers. But threats are just as real in the front-country. Every year, day visitors to both parks slip on rocks, trip on uneven surfaces, become dehydrated, suffer from too much sun, and have heart or breathing problems due to the extreme altitude. Use common sense, know your limitations, and don't be afraid to ask for help.

Bryce Canyon publishes a list of the top 10 causes for injuries in the park. These include unsafe driving, climbing or skiing off the canyon rim, feeding animals, ignoring extreme weather, dehydration, leaving the trail, over-exhaustion, and choosing the wrong footwear. Similar hazards have caused injuries at Zion, where flash floods and falls off cliffs have also led to fatalities.

✎ Immunizations

There are no immunization requirements for visitors traveling to the United States for tourism.

🛏 Lodging

IN ZION

It can be very difficult to score a reservation at the park's only hotel, Zion Lodge, which has around 120 rooms and cabins but often books up many months in advance. There are sometimes last-minute cancellations, however, so it's worth checking even if you're planning a spontaneous trip.

Just outside the park and within walking distance of the South Entrance, Springdale has quite a few hotels, most of them quite modern and comfortable (but also pretty expensive during the busier months). As you venture farther from the park, to Hurricane and St. George (which abounds with options), you'll generally find less expensive rates. To the east of Zion, Orderville has a few overnight options, and Kanab has a good selection of mostly moderate-priced hotels.

IN BRYCE CANYON

The Lodge at Bryce Canyon offers the only accommodations within the park, and they include both historic cabins and mid-20th-century motel-style rooms. The setting is spectacular, but as with Zion, rooms book up way in advance, so plan accordingly.

The park's closest community, Bryce Canyon City, has

Essentials

three lodgings, all of them quite expensive and only one (the Best Western Plus Bryce Canyon Grand) that's worth splurging on. In the surrounding area, within an hour or so of the park, you'll find a good mix of old-school budget motels, restored cabin compounds, rustic-chic glamping compounds, reliable chain properties, and upscale boutique inns. Kanab and Cedar City have the largest selection, but Panguitch, Tropic, and Escalante all have at least a few worthwhile lodgings.

FACILITIES

In most conventional hotels, rooms typically have private baths and usually TVs, phones, and air-conditioning, but the park lodges generally lack such amenities, as do some glamping spots and smaller properties. A handful of places include breakfast in their rates, and some of the larger accommodations—especially chain properties in Cedar City, Kanab, and St. George—have pools.

PARKING

Parking is typically free at the area's hotels.

PRICES

Rates at the park lodges and in hotels near the park run highest from late spring through early fall. In winter, hotel rates tend to drop by 20%–50%

(the Lodge at Bryce Canyon is closed in winter). One exception to this rule is the Brian Head area, where winter brings visitors who come to hit the slopes—the handful of lodgings there charge peak-season rates at that time. Smaller lodgings in some gateway towns sometimes close at least a couple of months in winter.

RESERVATIONS

For both Zion and Bryce, reserve rooms and campsites as far in advance as possible for stays in late spring through early autumn. If you're willing to stay upward of an hour away from the parks, you can usually score same-day reservations, especially in St. George, which has more than 65 lodgings.

What It Costs			
$	$$	$$$	$$$$
FOR TWO PEOPLE			
under $200	$200–$350	$351–$500	over $500

🧳 Packing

While it's best not to over pack, especially when heading into the parks via shuttles and out onto trails, it's important to be prepared for the weather and for both planned and spontaneous activities.

Sun protection is essential, including sun block, sunglasses, and hats. In summer, pack at least one lightweight rain jacket and a pair of long pants, especially if you plan to do any horseback riding. Capris, shorts, and zip-off pants are good options for hot days. Year-round but especially during the shoulder seasons, dressing in layers makes it easier to adapt to the region's often extreme temperature swings. In winter, particularly at Bryce Canyon, you'll need a warm waterproof jacket, knit hat, gloves, and long underwear. Sturdy footwear is necessary for nearly all activities. Also bring a pair of closed-toe water shoes (these can be rented from outfitters) for hiking up The Narrows or river rafting

A daypack is also a must (practice with it before traveling to make sure it's comfortable to carry). In addition to sunscreen and extra clothing layers, carry snacks and plenty of water: a gallon per person per day is recommended (you can fill up as needed when in developed areas, but don't head out to the backcountry with an empty bottle). On trips long or short, it's also good to have water-purification tablets, bug spray, a small first-aid kit, a flashlight, a camera, and lightweight binoculars. For longer treks, bring meals as well as snacks, a tablecloth, a head lamp and star chart if you plan to be out in the evening, and plastic bags to bring back garbage and used toilet paper (please don't leave it in the park!). Other handy things include a park guide and other special-interest books and small resealable plastic bags for protecting tech items in a sudden downpour or when trekking through rivers.

🌐 Passport

All visitors to the United States require a passport that is valid for six months beyond your expected period of stay.

🪪 Permits

In Zion and Bryce, permits are required for backcountry camping, and Zion also has permit requirements for certain other trails and climbs. Refer to the Permits section in each park's chapter for details.

💲 Taxes

Sales tax is 4.7% in Utah. Most areas have additional local sales and lodging taxes. For example, in St. George, the combined sales tax is 6.75%.

Essentials

Tipping Guides for Zion and Bryce Canyon

Bartender	$1–$5 per round of drinks, depending on the number of drinks
Bellhop	$1–$5 per bag, depending on the level of the hotel
Coat Check	$1–$2 per coat
Hotel Concierge	$5 or more, depending on the service
Hotel Doorstaff	$1–$5 for help with bags or hailing a cab
Hotel Housekeeping	$2–$5 a day (in cash, preferably daily since cleaning staff may be different each day you stay)
Hotel Room Service Waiter	$1–$2 per delivery, even if a service charge has been added
Porter at Airport or Train Station	$1 per bag
Restroom Attendant	$1 or small change
Skycap at Airport	$1–$3 per bag checked
Spa Personnel	15%–20% of the cost of your service
Taxi Driver	15%–20% of fare
Tour Guide	10%–15% of the cost of the tour, per person
Valet Parking Attendant	$2–$5, each time your car is brought to you
Waiter	15%–20%, with 20% being increasingly the norm; nothing additional if a service charge is added to the bill

💲 Tipping

At least 15% is customary in restaurants, but 20% is increasingly the norm. For coat checks and bellhops, $1 per coat or bag is the minimum.

Taxi and ride-share drivers expect 15%–20%. In resort towns, ski technicians, sandwich makers, baristas, and the like also appreciate tips.

🛂 Visa

Except for citizens of Canada and Bermuda, most visitors to the United States must have a visa. If you are from one of the 40 designated members of the Visa Waiver Program, then you only require an ESTA (Electronic System for Travel Authorization) as long as you are staying for 90 days or less.

📅 When to Go

Low Season: November through February is the low season at Zion, though the park gets a lot of visitors during the week from Christmas to New Year's (the park shuttle runs at this time as well). In smaller gateway towns, some accommodations and eateries shut down during this time. Low season at Bryce Canyon runs November through March, which is also when the Lodge at Bryce Canyon and park restaurants are closed.

Shoulder Season: Both parks are less crowded in the spring and fall, although from May and September through mid-October, the area has become increasingly popular (especially on weekends), and hotel rates tend to reflect this. Note that higher-elevation Bryce Canyon does get snow in early spring, so trails might still be covered.

High Season: From Memorial Day to Labor Day, the parks are busiest and offer the most activities. The gateway ski town of Brian Head, however, is busiest in winter.

WEATHER

Summer in Zion is hot and dry except for sudden cloudbursts, which can cause flash floods (but can also create spectacular waterfalls!). Expect afternoon thunderstorms between July and September. Even in the height of summer, there is ample shade on the canyon floor. Winters are mild at lower desert elevations, so consider planning a shoulder-season visit. Expect winter-driving conditions and very few park programs from November through March. Nevertheless, winter is a wonderful, solitary time to see the canyons.

Around Bryce Canyon National Park and the nearby Cedar Breaks National Monument area, elevations approach and surpass 9,000 feet, making for temperamental weather, intermittent and seasonal road closures, and downright cold nights well into June. At this altitude, the warm summer sun is perfectly balanced by the coolness of the alpine forests during the day. Bryce gets much more snow than Zion, so keep that in mind when you plan a winter trip.

On the Calendar

February

Bryce Canyon Winter Festival. Ruby's Inn hosts this three-day festival, held over Presidents' Day weekend, for snow lovers, featuring ski races, Nordic skiing tours, snowshoeing, archery, and stargazing. Inside, enjoy arts and crafts, photography workshops, yoga, dancing, and more. ⊕ *www.rubysinn.com/bryce-canyon-winter-festival*

Panguitch Lake Ice Fishing Derby. In early February, anglers fish for rainbow trout under thick ice and then take the fish they reel in to be weighed and measured for prizes. The hockey slapshot contest is another fun activity on the ice. ⊕ *panguitch.com/big-fish-ice-fishing-derby*

March

St. George Art Festival. Held the Friday and Saturday before Easter in St. George's Town Square, this popular festival has an artisan market, kids activities, food booths, and plenty of entertainment—from music to cowboy poetry. ⊕ *www.sgartfestival.com*

April

Concert in the Park. On the first Monday of the month, from April through September, St. George's Vernon Worthen Park hosts free, family-friendly concerts in the park. Bring a blanket (or get there a little early for park seating) and pick up dinner to go and join locals enjoying a relaxed musical Monday. ⊕ *www.sgcity.org/allartsandrecreation/concertinthepark*

May

Bryce Canyon Country Rodeo. Watch, or even ride in, the rodeo every Wednesday to Saturday throughout most of the summer at the Ruby's Inn rodeo grounds. ⊕ *www.rubysinn.com/activities-in-bryce-canyon/utah-rodeo*

Festival of the Americas. At the Kayenta Art Village, near ancestral lands of the Paiute, celebrate traditions of Native Americans, Latinos, and other early cultures in late May. There's music, theater, ethnic foods, artisans, and powwow activities like drumming circles and friendship dances. ⊕ *kayentaarts.org*

June

Bryce Canyon Astronomy Festival. Activities at this four-day, mid-June event include ranger talks, guided walks, and model-rocket building. In the evening, learn more about the night sky through telescopes. ⊕ *www.nps.gov/brca/planyourvisit/astrofest.htm*

Panguitch Valley Balloon Rally. Hot-air balloons fill the skies with color in this two-day, late-month event. At night, Main Street features a "balloon glow." ⊕ *panguitch.com/panguitch-valley-balloon-rally*

Quilt Walk Festival. One hard winter, early pioneers discovered they could travel to get food and supplies by laying down quilts to walk over heavy snow. A quilt show, pioneer-home tours, and more commemorate that historical event in Panguitch over four days in the second week in June. ⊕ *www.quiltwalk.org*

Utah Shakespeare Festival. It's been a Shakespeare extravaganza in Cedar City since 1962, with shows running from June through mid-October at three venues, including an open-air replica of the bard's Globe Theatre. ⊕ *www.bard.org*

July

Bryce Canyon Geology Festival (Geo Fest). Geologist-guided tours, exhibits, and plein air painting are some of the activities at this fun, informative, two-day festival held in mid-July. ⊕ *www.nps.gov/brca/annual-geology-festival.htm*

Utah Midsummer Renaissance Faire. Travel back to medieval times, with lively entertainment, unique wares, and hearty feasting fare at a four-day, mid-July event in Cedar City. ⊕ *umrf.net*

September

Dixie Roundup Rodeo. Put on your favorite cowboy or cowgirl attire and head to St. George's Sun Bowl for all the best in rodeo fun, from bull riding to mutton busting. The four-day event takes place the second week of the month. ⊕ *www.stgeorgelions.com*

Escalante Canyons Art Festival. Near the Grand Staircase–Escalante Monument, this art and literary gathering—held over two weeks, starting mid-month—highlights the area's history, paying tribute to the legendary young poet-artist Everett Ruess, who disappeared near here in 1934. ⊕ *escalantecanyonsartfestival.org*

On the Calendar

Zion Canyon Music Festival. The long-running, weekend festival is held late in the month at O.C. Tanner Amphitheater in Springdale, just minutes from the park entrance. Bands play folk, blues, rock, and more. ⊕ *zioncanyonmusicfestival.com*

October

Art in Kayenta. This three-day free annual festival, held at Kayenta Art Village, features the work of over 50 juried regional and national artists against the stunning desert backdrop. As well as spectacular art, you'll find a beer and wine garden, food vendors, and live music. ⊕ *kayentaarts.org/art-in-kayenta*

Cedar City Livestock & Heritage Festival. Celebrating all things agricultural, this two-day, late-month festival includes a sheep parade down Cedar City's main drag, a tractor-pull, a draft-horse show, a Dutch oven–cooking contest, cowboy poetry, and music. ⊕ *cedarlivestockfest.com*

Scarecrow Walk & Haunted Canyon. See scarecrows and walk through a canyon decorated with skeletons and other spooky things at St. George's Red Hills Desert Garden during the last three weeks of October. ⊕ *www.wcwcd.org/event/scarecrow-walk-haunted-canyon*

November

Holiday Lights at Red Hills Desert Garden. Beginning the night after Thanksgiving and running through New Year's Eve, the garden is filled with twinkling lights to celebrate the season. ⊕ *www.wcwcd.org/event/holiday-lights-at-red-hills-desert-garden*

December

Christmas Bird Count. Learn about the birds of Bryce Canyon, and become a citizen scientist by helping count them in the park the Saturday before Christmas. Coordinated by the Audubon Society, this event has been held nationwide since 1900. ⊕ *utahbirds.org/cbc/cbc.html*

Contacts

Air

AIRPORTS Cedar City Regional Airport. ✉ *2560 Aviation Way, Cedar City* ☎ *435/867-9408* ⊕ *www.cedarcity.org/2360/airport.* **Harry Reid International Airport (LAS).** ✉ *5757 Wayne Newton Blvd., Airport* ☎ *702/261-5211* ⊕ *www.harryreidairport.com.* **Salt Lake City International Airport (SLC).** ✉ *3920 W. Terminal Dr., Airport* ☎ *801/575-2400* ⊕ *www.slcairport.com.* **St. George Regional Airport (SGU).** ✉ *4550 S. Airport Pkwy., St. George* ☎ *435/627-1080* ⊕ *www.flysgu.com.*

AIRLINES American Airlines. ☎ *800/433-7300* ⊕ *www.aa.com.* **Delta Airlines.** ☎ *800/221-1212 for U.S. reservations, 800/241-4141 for international reservations* ⊕ *www.delta.com.* **United Airlines.** ☎ *000/004 0001 U.S. and Canada reservations* ⊕ *www.united.com.*

Bus

Greyhound. ☎ *800/231-2222* ⊕ *www.greyhound.com.* **National Park Express.** ☎ *702/903-2081* ⊕ *www.nationalparkexpress.com.* **St. George Shuttle.** ✉ *1275 E Red Hills Pkwy., St. George* ☎ *800/933-8320, 435/628-8320* ⊕ *www.stgshuttle.com.*

Zion Guru Shuttle. ✉ *Springdale* ☎ *432/632-0432* ⊕ *www.zionguru.com/hiking-shuttles.* **Zion Rock and Mountain Guides Shuttle.** ✉ *Springdale* ☎ *435/772-3303* ⊕ *www.zionrockguides.com.*

🚗 Car

ROAD CONDITIONS Nevada Department of Transportation. ☎ *511* ⊕ *www.nvroads.com.* **Utah Department of Transportation.** ☎ *511* ⊕ *udottraffic.utah.gov.*

🚆 Train

Amtrak. ☎ *800/872-7245* ⊕ *www.amtrak.com.*

Did You Know?

With multiple and surprisingly diverse ecosystems, Zion National Park contains roughly 85% of the flora and fauna that can be found throughout the state of Utah.

ZION NATIONAL PARK

Updated by
Andrew Collins

🏕 Camping	🛏 Hotels	🎽 Activities	👁 Scenery	👥 Crowds
★★★★★	★★★★☆	★★★★★	★★★★★	★☆☆☆☆

WELCOME TO ZION NATIONAL PARK

TOP REASONS TO GO

★ **Eye candy:** Just about every trail culminates in an astounding view of pink, orange, and crimson rock formations.

★ **Peace and quiet:** From March through November, cars aren't allowed on Zion Canyon Scenic Drive, so that section of the park stays relatively peaceful.

★ **Botanical wonderland:** Zion Canyon has over 1,000 species of plants, more than anywhere else in Utah.

★ **Animal tracks:** Zion's expansive hinterlands are full of furry, scaly, or feathered residents, such as deer, elk, lizards, and birds of prey.

★ **Unforgettable canyoneering:** Rugged slot canyons are perfect for scrambling, rappelling, climbing, and descending.

1 **Zion Canyon.** For most people, Zion is defined by this area, where the backcountry is accessible via the West Rim Trail and The Narrows and 2,000-foot cliffs rise all around.

2 **Kolob Canyons.** Zion's northwestern corner is a secluded 30,000-acre wonderland accessible only via a special entrance. Don't miss the West Temple and Kolob Arch.

The walls of Zion Canyon soar more than 2,000 feet above the valley, but it's the character, not the size, of the sandstone forms that defines the park's splendor. The domes, fins, and blocky massifs bear the names and likenesses of cathedrals and temples, prophets, and angels.

But for all Zion's grandeur, trails that lead deep into side canyons and up narrow ledges on the sheer canyon walls reveal a subtler beauty. Tucked among the monoliths are delicate hanging gardens, serene spring-fed pools, and shaded spots of solitude. So diverse is this place that 85% of Utah's flora and fauna species are found here. Some, like the tiny Zion snail, appear nowhere else in the world.

At the genesis of Zion is the Virgin River, a tributary of the mighty Colorado. It's hard to believe that this muddy stream is responsible for carving the great canyon you see, until you witness it transformed into a rumbling red torrent during spring runoff and summer thunderstorms. Cascades pour from the cliff tops, clouds float through the canyon, and then the sun comes out, and you know you're walking in one of the West's most loved and sacred places. If you're lucky, you may catch such a spectacle, but when the noisy waters run thick with debris, make sure that you keep a safe distance—these "flash floods" can, and do, kill.

The park comprises two distinct sections—Zion Canyon and the Kolob Plateau and Canyons. Most people restrict their visit to the better-known Zion Canyon, especially if they have only one day to explore, but the Kolob area has much to offer and should not be missed if time allows. There's little evidence of Kolob's beauty from the entrance point off Interstate 15, but once you negotiate the first switchback on the park road, you are hit with a vision of red rock cliffs shooting out of the earth. As you climb in elevation, you are treated first to a journey through these canyons, then with a view into the chasm. Due to geography—no roads connect Zion Canyon with Kolob Canyons—and to access points that are far apart, it is difficult to explore both sections in one day.

Great Itineraries

Zion in One Day

Begin your visit at the **Zion Canyon Visitor Center,** where outdoor exhibits inform you about the park's geology, wildlife, history, and trails. Get a taste of what's in store by viewing the far off Towers of the Virgin, then head to the **Court of the Patriarchs** viewpoint to take photos and walk the short path. Take the shuttle (or your car, if it's December or January) to **Zion Lodge,** and then make the easy hike to the **Grotto** and potentially a longer and more strenuous trek to **Scout Lookout,** which is on the West Trail as you approach the junction with the Angels Landing Trail, and is one of park's most stunning spots. Ride the next shuttle to the end of the road, where the paved, accessible **Riverside Walk,** Zion's most popular path, leads to the gateway of the canyon's **Narrows.**

Reboard the shuttle to return to the Zion Canyon Visitor Center to pick up your car. Head out onto the beautiful **Zion–Mount Carmel Highway,** with its long, curving tunnel. Turn around once you reach the park's East Entrance, and on your return trip stop to take the short hike up to **Canyon Overlook.** In the evening, attend a ranger program.

Zion in Three Days

Take at least one signature hike on Day 1.

Start Day 2 with a daybreak drive along the **Zion–Mt. Carmel Highway.** As the sun rises behind you, hike the short **Canyon Overlook Trail** to get some stunning pictures of Zion Canyon's south end. Return through the tunnel, leave your car at **Canyon Junction,** and take the shuttle all the way to the **Temple of Sinawava.** The **Riverside Walk** is a peaceful, mile-long, waterside wander that deposits you at the mouth of **The Narrows,** one of Zion's most famed attractions. Wade in and wander upriver. Whether you continue around one bend or for 5 miles, you'll be humbled by the surrounding 2,000-foot cliffs. The steep scramble up to legendary **Angels Landing** is another hugely rewarding option, but keep in mind that you must apply online for a mandatory permit (which is issued by lottery).

On Day 3, head north to **Kolob Canyons,** where the **Taylor Creek Trail** follows the riverbed past two homesteaders' cabins to the memorable **Double Arch Alcove.** This relatively flat hike also showcases an ever-narrowing "finger" canyon. From here, you can continue north to explore **Cedar City;** in summer, end the day here with a performance of the Utah Shakespeare Festival.

AVERAGE HIGH/LOW TEMPERATURES (FAHRENHEIT)					
Jan.	Feb.	Mar.	Apr.	May	June
52/29	57/31	63/36	73/43	83/52	93/60
July	Aug.	Sept.	Oct.	Nov.	Dec.
100/68	97/66	91/60	78/49	63/37	53/30

Planning

When to Go

Zion is the most heavily visited national park in Utah, receiving 4.5 million visitors each year. Spring and fall used to be considered the shoulder seasons because traffic would drop off from the highly visited summer months. Not so much anymore. These days the park is extremely busy from March through November.

Summer in the park is hot and dry, punctuated by sudden cloudbursts that can create flash flooding and spectacular waterfalls. Expect afternoon thunderstorms between July and September. Whether the day starts out sunny or not, wear sunscreen and drink lots of water, even if you aren't exerting yourself or spending much time outside. The sun is very powerful at this elevation.

Winters are mild at lower desert elevations. You can expect to encounter winter driving conditions from November to mid-March, and although many park programs are suspended in winter, it is a wonderful and solitary time to see the canyons.

■ TIP→ The temperature in Zion often exceeds 100°F in July and August.

Getting Here and Around

AIR

The nearest commercial airport, with direct flights to Salt Lake City, Phoenix, and Denver, is an hour away in St. George; the tiny Cedar City Regional Airport also has twice-daily direct flights to Salt Lake City. It's about a 3-hour drive to the nearest major airport, Harry Reid International in Las Vegas, Nevada, and a 4½-hour drive to Salt Lake City's airport.

BUS

Greyhound buses run to the gateway city of St. George. From there, St. George Shuttle offers bus service to the park. In addition, National Park Express offers bus service directly to the park from Las Vegas, about 3 hours away; these buses also run from Zion to Bryce Canyon National Park.

From March through November, you can explore the park's central points of interest via the free Zion Canyon Line shuttle bus (private cars are not permitted on Zion Canyon Scenic Drive during these months), which leaves from the visitor center. From throughout the town of Springdale, the park's free Springdale Line shuttle runs to the park entrance, from which it's a short walk to the Zion Canyon Visitor Center. Especially during the busy late spring–early fall season, parking at your Springdale hotel or in one of the town's paid lots or street spaces and taking the shuttle into the park is a smart idea, as the parking lot at the visitor center often fills up early in the day.

Zion's quiet, propane powered shuttle buses serve the most visited portions in the Zion Canyon area. They run daily from March through November, as well as during the December holiday period. A couple of private companies, including Zion Guru and Zion Rock and Mountain Guides, offer private shuttle van service from Springdale into the more remote parts of Zion not served by the free park shuttles, such as the East Rim, Kolob Terrace Road, and Kolob Canyons; rates start around $200 one-way for up to four people.

CAR

Zion National Park lies 21 miles east of Interstate 15, via Highway 9, in southwestern Utah; the park's South Entrance (aka Main Entrance) is within walking distance of downtown Springdale.

From March through November, visitors are not permitted to drive on Zion Canyon Scenic Drive except for overnight guests of Zion Lodge traveling to and from the hotel. Otherwise, during this period, you must park your car in Springdale or at the Zion Canyon Visitor Center and take the free shuttle. During the ride, you'll hear an 18-minute narrated tour, which you can also listen to or download from the park website. Shuttles are accessible and have plenty of room for gear. Consult the print park guide or check online for updated shuttle schedules (⊕ *www.nps.gov/zion*).

Taking the park shuttle is a relaxing way to enjoy Zion Canyon views.

You'll need a car to reach and explore Kolob Canyons in the park's northwest corner. ⚠ **For much of 2023, Kolob Canyons Road was closed to vehicles beyond South Fork Picnic Area (a little over a mile past the Taylor Creek Trailhead) due to significant road repairs. Confirm the road is open before you visit. Note that you can still bike or hike the final 2½ miles to the end of the road and its trailheads.** You'll also need a car to drive the breathtaking Zion–Mt. Carmel Highway. The mile-long tunnel has size restrictions and escort requirements for oversize vehicles, such as RVs (you'll need to pay a $15 permit fee, in addition to the park entrance fee); check the park website prior to your arrival.

Just outside the park in nearby Springdale, you can fuel up, get your tires and oil changed, and have auto repairs done.

Inspiration

A Zion Canyon Reader, edited by Nathan N. Waite and Reid L. Neilson, is a collection of short essays both historical and recent that cover the region's exploration and development, unique features, and personal meaning to the writers. It includes pieces by John Wesley Powell, Clarence Dutton, Everett Ruess, Edward Abbey, Wallace Stegner, and Juanita Brooks, whose own books provide further inspiration.

Zion, by Tamra Orr, is a great introduction to the park for elementary-school kids. Part of a series titled "A True Book: National Parks," it covers the park's history, geology, scenery, plants, and animals. Get the companion books on Bryce and the Grand Canyon if your family plans to visit those parks, too.

Zion National Park: Sanctuary in the Desert, by Nicky Leach, provides a photographic overview and a narrative journey through the park. Published by the Zion National Park Forever Project (⊕ *zionpark.org*), this book and others are available through the organization's online store as well as from major booksellers. The organization has three stores inside the park.

Park Essentials

ACCESSIBILITY
Both visitor centers, the Zion Human History Museum, all shuttle buses, and Zion Lodge are fully accessible to people in wheelchairs. Several campsites at Watchman Campground and South Campground offer accessible sites, but only Watchman Campground has accessible restrooms—there's a paved 1,500-foot path connecting the two areas. Two trails—Riverside Walk and Pa'rus Trail—are wheelchair-accessible, although they're best undertaken with some assistance. Service dogs are permitted on a leash throughout the park. Ranger-led programs are accessible; if you need an American Sign Language interpreter, contact a ranger in advance of your visit at ✉ *zion_park_information@nps.gov.*

CELL PHONE RECEPTION
Reception is good in Springdale and at the park entrances but spotty within the park, especially within canyons and other lower elevations. There's free public Wi-Fi at the Zion Canyon Visitor Center and the Zion Human History Museum.

PARK FEES AND PERMITS
The entrance fee for Zion National Park is $35 per vehicle, $30 per motorcycle, and $20 per person entering on foot or by bicycle and is good for seven days.

Permits are required for backcountry camping and overnight hikes as well as for hiking to Angels Landing. Canyoneering permits are required for parts of certain trails, including The Narrows and The Subway.

Zion limits the number of overnight and canyoneering permits issued per day; you must apply online, and a lottery system is in place during the April–October high season. Permits cost $15 for parties of up to two people, $20 for three to seven people, and $25 for 8 to 12 people (the maximum size for any group).

You can obtain a mandatory Angels Landing permit by applying for one of the quarterly seasonal lotteries or by applying for one of the daily permits released the day before you hike. The nonrefundable online application costs $6 (for up to six people in your party); if you are awarded a permit, each person in your party will pay an additional $3 for the permit itself.

PARK HOURS
The park, open daily year-round, 24 hours a day, is in the Mountain Time Zone.

Hotels

The only hotel within the park, Zion Lodge is rustic and comfortable, and was rebuilt in 1966 following a fire but in classic 1920s-period style. Just outside the main park entrance, Springdale has dozens of lodging options, from cozy boutique inns to midrange chain hotels to upscale retreats with lavish riverside rooms. Farther west you'll find a few more options in Hurricane and a great array of choices in St. George; rates tend to be lower in these areas and in general as you get farther from the park. To the east and north, you'll find a smattering of hotels, motels, and glamping compounds just beyond the park's East Entrance and then from Kanab up to Panguitch. These areas make useful bases if you're continuing on to Bryce or, in the case of Kanab, the North Rim of the Grand Canyon.

Restaurants

Only one full-service restaurant (at the famed Zion Lodge) operates within the park, but in Springdale, just outside the South (Main) Entrance, you'll find a bounty of mostly casual eateries, along with a few more sophisticated restaurants. To the east, there are a handful of options within an hour's drive, with the greatest concentration in Kanab.

⇨ *Hotel and restaurant reviews have been shortened. For full information, visit Fodors.com. Restaurant prices are the average cost of a main course at dinner, or if dinner is not served, at lunch. Hotel prices are the lowest cost of a standard double room in high season.*

What It Costs			
$	$$	$$$	$$$$
RESTAURANTS			
under $20	$20–$30	$31–$40	over $40
HOTELS			
under $200	$200–$350	$351–$500	over $500

Tours

★ Ranger-Guided Shuttle Tours

GUIDED TOURS | FAMILY | Departing from the Zion Canyon Visitor Center daily at 9 am, from late May through September, rangers conduct free two-hour shuttle tours of points of interest along Zion Canyon Scenic Drive. In addition to learning about the canyon's geology, ecology, and history, you'll be treated to some great photo ops. Reservations are required and can be made in person at the visitor center up to three days in advance. ⊠ *Zion National Park* ⊕ *www.nps.gov/zion/planyourvisit/ranger-led-activities.htm.*

★ Ranger-Led Hikes

WALKING TOURS | FAMILY | Guided hikes along the 3½-mile Watchman Trail provide an overview of the park's geology and natural and other history. You must sign up the day before at the Zion Canyon Visitor Center, from which these hikes depart daily at 8 am from June through August. ⊠ *Zion National Park* ⊕ *www.nps.gov/zion/planyourvisit/ranger-led-activities.htm.*

Visitor Information

PARK CONTACT INFORMATION Zion National Park. ⊠ *1 Zion Park Blvd., off Hwy. 9, Springdale* ☎ *435/772–3256* ⊕ *www.nps.gov/zion.*

Zion Canyon

Although this area comprising the soaring 6-mile main canyon cut by the Virgin River as well as the Upper East Canyon along Highway 9 makes up only the southeastern third of Zion National Park, it's where the vast majority of the 4.5 million annual visitors spend their visits. There's no denying the beauty and scale of the solid rock cliffs that dwarf the stream-fed valley below—indeed, this part of the park is so popular because it contains some of its most well-known attractions and hikes, from Angels Landing and The Court of the Patriarchs to Zion Lodge and Canyon Overlook.

Zion Canyon is also easy to access and contains the park's main visitor center, which sits right at the border with the cute town of Springdale, an excellent base with plenty of lodging and dining options. Highway 9 (aka Zion–Mt. Carmel Highway) traverses this portion of the park from the South Entrance (sometimes referred to as the Main Entrance) in Springdale through the dramatic Zion–Mt. Carmel Tunnel to the East Entrance. You can drive this road year-round, and you'll find plenty of pullouts for hopping out, stretching your legs, and snapping photos; several popular trailheads are located along here, too.

The most spectacular section of the main canyon is accessed via spectacular Zion Canyon Scenic Drive, but from about March through November (check the visitor center or park website for exact hours), you can only visit this road by free shuttle bus—unless you're overnighting at Zion Lodge, in which case you can drive your own car to that point. You'll find trailheads to several legendary hikes along this drive.

It's a good idea to bring insect repellent, as the trails along the Virgin River can get buggy from spring through early fall. Note, also, that the hikes from the canyon to Hidden Canyon and Observation Point were closed due to a major rock slide in 2019, and as of this writing, no reopening date has been announced. Check with the visitor center for further updates, or for advice on how to hike to Observation Point the much longer back way (via the East Mesa Trail).

◉ Sights

GEOLOGICAL LANDMARKS
★ The Narrows
NATURE SIGHT | This sinuous, 16-mile crack in the earth where the Virgin River flows over gravel and boulders is one of the world's most stunning gorges. If you hike through it, you'll find yourself

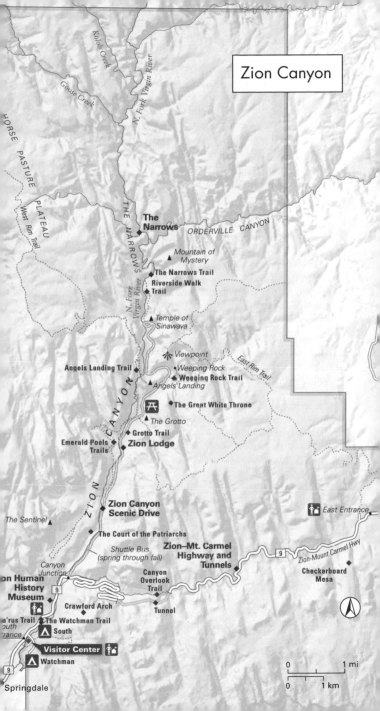

Zion Canyon

Kolob Creek

Goose Creek

N. Fork Virgin River

HORSE PASTURE PLATEAU

West Rim Trail

THE NARROWS

The Narrows

ORDERVILLE CANYON

Mountain of Mystery

The Narrows Trail
Riverside Walk Trail

N. Fork Virgin River

▲ *Temple of Sinawava*

☀ *Viewpoint*

East Rim Trail

Angels Landing Trail

• *Weeping Rock*
Weeping Rock Trail

Angels Landing

ZION CANYON

⌂ **The Great White Throne**

▲ *The Grotto*

Grotto Trail

Emerald Pools Trails ◆ **Zion Lodge**

Zion Canyon Scenic Drive

▲ *The Sentinel*

◆ **The Court of the Patriarchs**

Shuttle Bus (spring through fall)

Zion–Mt. Carmel Highway and Tunnels

⟨9⟩ *Zion-Mount Carmel Hwy*

Checkerboard Mesa

Canyon Junction

⟨9⟩

Canyon Overlook Trail

⌂ *East Entrance*

on Human History Museum

a'rus Trail
outh rance

◆ **Crawford Arch**

The Watchman Trail

▲ **South**

Tunnel

Visitor Center 🚹

▲ **Watchman**

⟨9⟩

Springdale

0 — 1 mi
0 — 1 km

surrounded—sometimes nearly boxed in—by smooth walls stretching high into the heavens. Plan to get wet, and be aware that deadly flash floods can occur here, especially in spring and summer. Always check on the weather before you enter, especially in spring when The Narrows has historically been closed for several weeks at a time due to high water levels. ✛ *Begins at Riverside Walk, at end of Zion Canyon Scenic Drive.*

HISTORIC SIGHTS

Zion Human History Museum

HISTORY MUSEUM | This informative museum tells the park's story from the perspective of its human inhabitants, among them Ancestral Puebloans and early Mormon settlers. Permanent exhibits illustrate how humans have dealt with wildlife, plants, and natural forces. Temporary exhibits have touched on everything from vintage park-employee photography to the history of Union Pacific Railroad hotels. Don't miss the incredible view of Towers of the Virgin from the back patio. ⊠ *Zion Canyon Scenic Dr., ½ mile north of South Entrance* ☎ *435/772–3256* ⊕ *www.nps.gov/zion* ▧ *Free.*

★ Zion Lodge

HOTEL | Architect Gilbert Stanley Underwood, responsible for many noteworthy national park lodges, designed the original Zion Lodge, which opened in 1924 but was destroyed by fire four decades later (the neighboring guest cabins survived and are still in use today). It was hastily rebuilt in about 100 days, and then in 1990, it received a painstaking restoration that brought it back to its original rustic style, in some cases down to the very paint color. Natural beauty is on display inside and out, from the lobby's rock columns and exposed wood to the cottonwoods shading the sprawling lawn. The main building includes a gift shop, an upscale restaurant, and an outdoor café with a large patio and beer garden. One way to experience the lodge and its surroundings is through an open-air narrated tram ride (the fare is $17). ⊠ *Zion Canyon Scenic Dr., Zion National Park* ☎ *435/772–7700* ⊕ *www. zionlodge.com.*

PICNIC AREAS

The Grotto

NATURE SIGHT | **FAMILY** | You can pick up food to go at nearby Zion Lodge or pack your own meal and take a short walk to this sheltered retreat shaded by tall oak trees. Amenities include drinking water, picnic tables, and restrooms, but there are no fire grates. You can access the Emerald Pools Trail from here. ⊠ *Off Zion Canyon Scenic Dr. at the Grotto, Zion National Park.*

Did You Know?

A hike through the waters of the Virgin River—a great way to cool off on a hot day—is required to access the gorge known as The Narrows.

SCENIC DRIVES
★ Zion Canyon Scenic Drive
SCENIC DRIVE | FAMILY | Vividly colored cliffs tower 2,000 feet above the road that meanders north from Highway 9 at Canyon Junction along the floor of Zion Canyon. As you roll through the narrow, steep canyon, you'll pass The Court of the Patriarchs, The Sentinel, and The Great White Throne, among other imposing rock formations. From roughly March through November, unless you're staying at the lodge, you can access Zion Canyon Scenic Drive only by riding the park shuttle. The rest of the year, you can drive it yourself. ⊠ *Off Hwy. 9 at Canyon Junction.*

Zion–Mt. Carmel Highway and Tunnels
SCENIC DRIVE | Two narrow tunnels as old as the park itself lie between the East Entrance and Zion Canyon on this breathtaking 12-mile stretch of Highway 9. One was once the longest man-made tunnel in the world. As you travel the (1.1-mile) passage through solid rock, five arched portals along one side provide fleeting glimpses of cliffs and canyons. When you emerge, you'll find that the landscape has changed dramatically. Large vehicles require traffic control and a $15 permit, available at either park entrance, and have restricted hours of travel. This includes nearly all RVs, trailers, dual-wheel trucks, and campers. The Canyon Overlook Trail starts from a parking area between the tunnels. ⊠ *Hwy. 9, 5 miles east of Canyon Junction* ⊕ *www.nps.gov/zion/planyourvisit/the-zion-mount-carmel-tunnel.htm.*

SCENIC STOPS
Checkerboard Mesa
NATURE SIGHT | It's well worth stopping at the pull-out 1 mile west of Zion's East Entrance to observe the distinctive waffle patterns on this huge white mound of sandstone. The stunning crosshatch effect visible today is the result of eons of freeze-and-thaw cycles that caused vertical fractures, combined with erosion that produced horizontal bedding planes. ⊠ *Hwy. 9.*

The Court of the Patriarchs
NATURE SIGHT | This trio of peaks bears the names of, from left to right, Abraham, Isaac, and Jacob. Mt. Moroni is the reddish peak on the far right that partially blocks the view of Jacob. Hike the trail that leaves from The Court of the Patriarchs viewpoint, 1½ miles north of Canyon Junction, to get a much better view of the sandstone prophets. ⊠ *Zion Canyon Scenic Dr.*

Crawford Arch
VIEWPOINT | From the north end of the parking lot at the Zion Human History Museum, look for a display pointing out an arch high on the western slope of the opposing hill. Crawford Arch is

Spend an hour or half a day exploring the lower, middle, and/or upper Emerald Pools.

just to the right of a saddle slope in the ridge—an easy one to view if you're keeping a "collection" of arches seen or visited in Utah. ⊠ *Zion Canyon Scenic Dr., Zion National Park.*

The Great White Throne
NATURE SIGHT | Dominating the Grotto picnic area near Zion Lodge, this massive Navajo sandstone peak juts 2,000 feet above the valley floor. The popular formation lies about 3 miles north of Canyon Junction. ⊠ *Zion Canyon Scenic Dr., Zion National Park.*

TRAILS
★ Angels Landing Trail
TRAIL | As much a trial as a trail, this serpentine path beneath The Great White Throne, which you access from the Lower West Rim Trail, is one of the park's most challenging and genuinely thrilling hikes. It had also been on the verge of becoming a victim of its own popularity, suffering badly from overcrowding, until the park service instituted a permit system in 2022, which has greatly reduced the number of hikers at any given time and vastly improved the experience. You now must apply online at ⊕ *www. recreation.gov* (both seasonal and day-before lotteries are held, and the cost is $6) for the chance to hike the famed final section beyond Scout Lookout.

Once you've ascended from the Lower West Rim Trail, you'll encounter Walter's Wiggles, an arduous (but not at all scary) series of 21 switchbacks built out of sandstone blocks that leads up to Scout Lookout. From here, assuming you've secured a permit,

Did You Know?

Zion's formations have up to nine layers (try counting them at vistas like this one!) of sedimentary rock deposited between 100 and 270 million years ago.

you'll continue along a narrow, steadily rising ridge with sheer cliffs that drop some 1,400 feet on either side. Chains bolted into the rock face serve as handrails in the steepest places. In spite of its hair-raising nature, and taking into consideration that 14 people have fallen to their deaths on this hike since 2000, the climb doesn't require technical skills and is quite safe as long as you step deliberately and use the handrail chains. Still, children and those uneasy about heights should not attempt this hike. Allow 2½ hours round-trip to hike to Scout Lookout (2 miles), which is itself an impressive viewpoint, and four to five hours if you continue to where the angels (and birds of prey) play. The total hike is about 4.5 miles round-trip from the Grotto shuttle stop. *Difficult.* ✛ *Trailhead: Off Zion Canyon Scenic Dr. at the Grotto* ⊕ *www.nps. gov/zion/planyourvisit/angels-landing-hiking-permits.htm.*

★ Canyon Overlook Trail

TRAIL | FAMILY | The parking area just east of the Zion–Mt. Carmel Tunnel leads to this highly popular trail, which is about 1 mile round-trip and takes about an hour to finish. From the breathtaking overlook at the trail's end, you can see the West and East Temples, Towers of the Virgin, The Streaked Wall, and other Zion Canyon cliffs and peaks. The elevation change is 160 feet. There's no shuttle to this trail, and the parking area often fills up—try to come very early or late in the day to avoid crowds. *Easy–Moderate.* ✛ *Trailhead: Off Hwy. 9 just east of Zion–Mt. Carmel Tunnel.*

Emerald Pools Trail

TRAIL | FAMILY | Multiple waterfalls cascade (or drip, in dry weather) into algae-filled pools along this trail that begins along the Virgin River on Zion Canyon Scenic Drive. (The path leading to the lower pool is paved but is too steep and narrow to be appropriate for wheelchairs, at least not without assistance.) If you've got any energy left, keep going past the lower pool. The ½ mile from there to the middle and then upper pools becomes rocky and somewhat steep but offers increasingly scenic views. A less crowded and exceptionally enjoyable return route follows the Kayenta Trail, connecting to the Grotto Trail. Allow 50 minutes for the 1¼-mile round-trip hike to the lower pool, and an hour more each round-trip to the middle (2 miles) and upper pools (3 miles). *Lower, easy. Upper and Middle, moderate.* ✛ *Trailhead: Off Zion Canyon Scenic Dr., at Zion Lodge or the Grotto.*

Grotto Trail

TRAIL | FAMILY | This level, 1-mile round-trip trail takes you from Zion Lodge to the lovely, tree-shaded Grotto picnic area, traveling much of the way parallel to the park road. Allow 20 minutes or less for this easy stroll through meadows and beneath a light tree canopy.

From here, you can cross the footbridge over the Virgin River to connect with the Kayenta Trail, which leads south to the Emerald Pools trails or north to the West Rim Trail and eventually up to Angels Landing (for which a permit is required). *Easy.* ✛ *Trailhead: Off Zion Canyon Scenic Dr. at the Grotto.*

★ The Narrows Trail

TRAIL | After leaving the paved ease of the Riverside Walk (aka the Gateway to The Narrows Trail) behind, this famous and challenging trek entails walking on the riverbed itself. You'll find a pebbly shingle or dry sandbar path, but when the walls of the canyon close in, you'll be forced into the chilly waters of the Virgin River. A walking stick and proper water shoes are a must. Be prepared to swim, as chest-deep holes may occur even when water levels are low. More than half of the entire hike takes place at least partially wading or even possibly swimming in the water, but the views of the sheer canyon walls are something else. Always check the weather forecast and with park rangers about the likelihood of flash floods—hikers died on two occasions in 2022, one by being swept away after a sudden thunderstorm and the other from hypothermia. A day trip up the lower section of The Narrows is about 4.7 miles one-way to the turnaround point at Big Spring. Allow at least five to seven hours round-trip. *Difficult.* ✛ *Trailhead: Off Zion Canyon Scenic Dr., at end of Riverside Walk.*

The Narrows Trail (From the Top)

TRAIL | "From the Top" means shuttling out to Chamberlain's Ranch, which is slightly northeast of the park boundary, and following the canyon for 16 miles to the Temple of Sinawava. A canyoneering permit is required to undertake this dramatic trek, which can be done in one very long day, but most hikers overnight at one of 12 backcountry campsites located roughly midway through the hike. You'll have to rappel down 12-foot waterfalls and wander through miles of river, and you can explore multiple side canyons. On the plus side, it's all downhill! Ropes and rappelling equipment are required, as are backcountry permits. Several local outfitters offer shuttle service to Chamberlain's Ranch as well as guided hikes; if you're driving to the trailhead, you can get directions when you pick up your permit (this must be done in person) at the visitor center. *Difficult.* ✉ *Chamberlain's Ranch, Zion National Park* ✛ *About 18 miles north of Hwy. 9, northeast of the park boundary* ⊕ *https://www.nps.gov/zion/planyourvisit/thenarrows.htm.*

Pa'rus Trail

TRAIL | **FAMILY** | This relatively flat, paved walking and biking path parallels and occasionally crosses the Virgin River and offers a great way to take in some of Zion Canyon's most impressive

Did You Know?

The Angels Landing Trail's 21 switchbacks are called "Walter's Wiggles," as Walter Ruesch, Zion's first superintendent, was responsible for creating them in 1926.

vistas while using a wheelchair or stroller, spending time with your pooch (leashed dogs are welcome), or simply enjoying a relaxing ramble or bike ride. Starting at South Campground, ½ mile north of the South Entrance, the walk proceeds north along the river to the beginning of Zion Canyon Scenic Drive and is 3.5 miles round-trip. Along the way you'll take in great views of The Watchman, The Sentinel, the East and West Temples, and Towers of the Virgin. Keep an eye out for bicycles zipping by. *Easy.* ✛ *Trailhead: At South Campground.*

Riverside Walk

TRAIL | FAMILY | This 2.2-mile round-trip hike that's also sometimes referred to as the Gateway to The Narrows Trail shadows the Virgin River. In spring, wildflowers bloom on the opposite canyon wall in lovely hanging gardens. The trail, which begins at the end of Zion Canyon Scenic Drive, is one of the park's most visited, so be prepared for crowds. The Riverside Walk is paved and suitable for strollers and wheelchairs, though some wheelchair users may need assistance. Round-trip it takes about 90 minutes. At the end, The Narrows Trail—which is much more challenging—begins. *Easy.* ✛ *Trailhead: Off Zion Canyon Scenic Dr. at the Temple of Sinawava.*

The Watchman Trail

TRAIL | FAMILY | For a dramatic view of Springdale and a great introduction to the park's landscape, including lower Zion Creek Canyon and Towers of the Virgin, this moderately taxing adventure begins on a service road east of Watchman Campground. Some springs seep out of the sandstone, nourishing the hanging gardens and attracting wildlife. There are a few sheer cliff edges, so supervise children carefully. Plan on two hours to complete this nearly 3½-mile round-trip hike with a 368-foot elevation change. *Moderate.* ✛ *Trailhead: At Zion Canyon Visitor Center.*

Weeping Rock Trail

TRAIL | FAMILY | A half-mile round-trip, this is definitely a kid-friendly trail. Hop off the bus three stops from the north end of the park. The well-marked trail is shaded and has a steady incline that leads to steps as you approach the alcove. Although much of the trail is paved, the steepness and irregularity may make it difficult for strollers and wheelchairs. Amaze your kids when you tell them the water trickling down on them has taken more than 1,000 years to seep down and through Echo Canyon. *Easy.* ✉ *Zion Canyon Scenic Dr., Zion Canyon, Zion National Park* ✛ *4 miles north of Canyon Junction.*

Extraordinary canyon views are the reward for hiking the 8-mile round-trip Observation Trail.

VISITOR CENTERS

Zion Canyon Visitor Center

VISITOR CENTER | **FAMILY** | Learn about the area's geology, flora, and fauna at the outdoor interpretive exhibits next to a gurgling stream. Inside, a large shop sells everything from field guides to souvenirs. Zion Canyon shuttle buses leave regularly from the center, which is just a five-minute walk from Zion Canyon Village, from which you can pick up the Springdale Line shuttle bus. Ranger-guided shuttle tours depart once a day from late May through September. Within a short walk you can also access the small Zion Nature Center, the park's two main campgrounds, and both The Watchman and Pa'rus hiking trails. During busy periods, the visitor center and surrounding plaza can feel like a bit of a zoo (and spaces can be tough to come by in the parking lot); try to arrive very early or late in the day if you can. ✉ *Zion Park Blvd. at South Entrance* ☎ *435/772–3256* ⊕ *www.nps.gov/zion.*

🍴 Restaurants

Castle Dome Café

$ | **CAFÉ** | Next to the shuttle stop at Zion Lodge, this small, convenient, fast-food restaurant has a lovely shaded patio but no indoor seating. You can grab a banana, burger, smoothie, or salad to go, order local brews from the beer garden cart, or enjoy a dish of ice cream while soaking up the views of the surrounding geological formations. **Known for:** quick option for pre- or posthiking; gorgeous views; nice beer selection. **⑤** *Average main: $8*

✉ *Zion Lodge, Zion Canyon Scenic Dr.* ☎ *435/772–7700* ⊕ *www. zionlodge.com* ☉ *Closed Dec.–late Feb. No dinner.*

Red Rock Grill

$$ | AMERICAN | The dinner fare at this restaurant in Zion Lodge includes steaks, seafood, and Western specialties, such as pecan-encrusted trout and garlic-rubbed sirloin steaks with a cranberry-wine sauce; salads, sandwiches, and hearty Navajo tacos are lunch highlights; and, for breakfast, you can partake of the plentiful buffet. Photos showcasing the surrounding landscape adorn the walls of the spacious dining room; enormous windows and a large patio (which can be buggy) take in the actual landscape. **Known for:** there can be a wait for a table at busy times; astounding canyon views from dining room and patio; only full-service restaurant in the park. ⑤ *Average main: $20* ✉ *Zion Lodge, Zion Canyon Scenic Dr.* ☎ *435/772–7760* ⊕ *www.zionlodge.com.*

🛏 Hotels

★ Zion Lodge

$$ | HOTEL | For a dramatic setting inside the park, you'd be hard-pressed to improve on a stay at the historic Zion Lodge: the canyon's jaw-dropping beauty surrounds you, access to trailheads is easy, and guests can drive their cars on the lower half of Zion Canyon Scenic Drive year-round. **Pros:** ideal location if planning a long day hike in the canyon; incredible views; home to the park's only restaurants. **Cons:** pathways are dimly lit; spotty Wi-Fi, poor cell service; books up months ahead. ⑤ *Rooms from: $245* ✉ *Zion Canyon Scenic Dr.* ☎ *888/297–2757, 435/772–7700* ⊕ *www. zionlodge.com* ⇌ *122 rooms* ⑩ *No Meals.*

🛍 Shopping

Zion Canyon Visitor Center Store

SOUVENIRS | The comprehensive shop operated by the Zion National Park Forever Project is located at the main visitor center and sells maps and travel books, puzzles, jewelry, apparel, Native American crafts, and light hiking gear. ✉ *South Entrance, Zion National Park* ☎ *435/772–3264* ⊕ *www.zionpark.org.*

Zion Lodge Gift Shop

SOUVENIRS | The lodge's gift shop has everything from nature books and hiking gear to Native American jewelry and leather goods. ✉ *Zion Canyon Scenic Dr., Zion National Park* ☎ *435/772–7700.*

Kolob Canyons

Overlooked by many park visitors, Kolob Canyons and Kolob Terrace offer windows into an entirely different habitat from that of Zion Canyon. About 45 minutes from Springdale, the Kolob Canyons section showcases the red rocks of the park's northwest corner. It's accessible from I–15 at Exit 40, and nothing in the appearance of the unassuming visitor center here hints at the lush red canyons that cut into the mountains behind it. The entire 5-mile road is within park boundaries, with two trailheads offering day hikes and one trailhead leading into the vast backcountry. △ **A rockslide precipitated by major winter storms closed part of the road in early 2023. As of this writing, the road was closed to vehicular traffic for roughly the final 2½ miles, beyond South Fork Picnic Area; repairs may continue well into 2024, so check the park website for updates. Fortunately, visitors can still hike or bike the road all the way to the end, at Kolob Canyons Viewpoint—and it's a beautiful, if slightly hilly, walk.**

Farther south, Kolob Terrace Road runs to lava fields, a reservoir, and a beautiful campground, Lava Point, in the heart of the park's backcountry. Unlike Kolob Canyons Road, much of this road is outside park boundaries, hopscotching through Bureau of Land Management and private land. Look for evidence of prehistoric volcanic activity, with black rock prevailing here rather than the red clay and white sandstone that characterizes much of the rest of the park. There are a number of noteworthy peaks to see, several trailheads through which to access the backcountry, and, finally, Kolob Reservoir, which has somewhat low water levels, due to drought in recent years.

◉ Sights

PICNIC AREAS
★ Kolob Canyons Viewpoint
VIEWPOINT | FAMILY | The big payoff for entering the northwestern Kolob Canyons section of the park off Interstate 15, this spectacular viewpoint lies at the end of 5-mile Kolob Canyons Road (note that the final 2½ miles of road are closed to vehicles for road repairs until at least early 2024, but you can still access the viewpoint on foot or by bike). You'll be treated to a beautiful view of Kolob's "finger" canyons from the several picnic tables spread out beneath the trees. The parking lot has plenty of spaces, a pit toilet, and an overlook with a display pointing out the area's most prominent geological features. Restrooms and drinking water

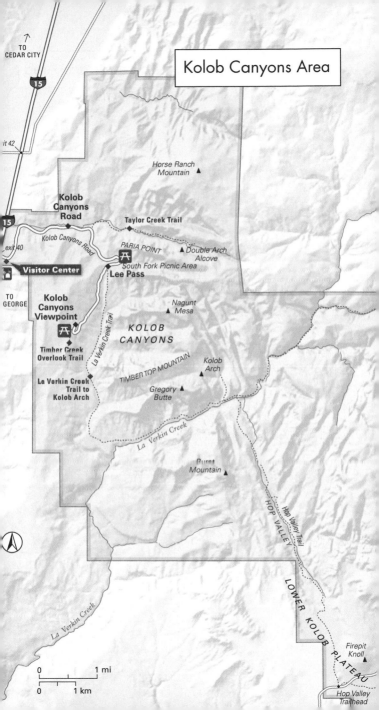

Kolob Canyons Area

TO CEDAR CITY

I-15

it 42

exit 40

Horse Ranch Mountain

Kolob Canyons Road

Taylor Creek Trail

Kolob Canyons Road

I-15

PARIA POINT

Double Arch Alcove

Visitor Center

South Fork Picnic Area

Lee Pass

TO GEORGE

Kolob Canyons Viewpoint

Nagunt Mesa

KOLOB CANYONS

Timber Creek Overlook Trail

La Verkin Creek Trail

TIMBER TOP MOUNTAIN

Kolob Arch

La Verkin Creek Trail to Kolob Arch

Gregory Butte

La Verkin Creek

Burnt Mountain

HOP VALLEY

Hop Valley Trail

LOWER KOLOB PLATEAU

La Verkin Creek

Firepit Knoll

Hop Valley Trailhead

0   1 mi

0   1 km

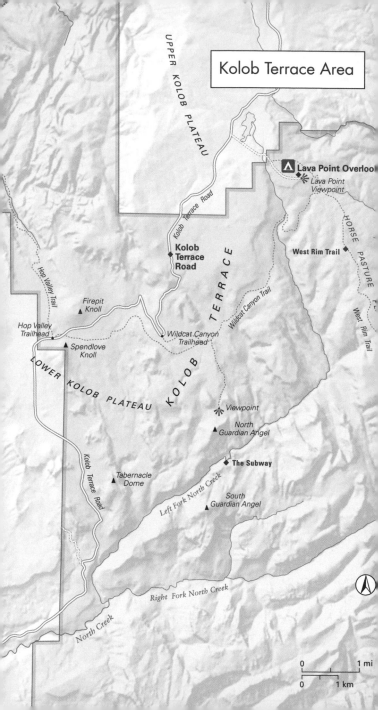

are available at the start of the drive, at the Kolob Canyons Visitor Center. ✛ *End of Kolob Canyons Rd.*

SCENIC DRIVES
★ Kolob Canyons Road
SCENIC DRIVE | Receiving relatively little traffic, Kolob Canyons Road climbs 5 miles into red rock canyons that extend east-to-west along three forks of Taylor Creek and La Verkin Creek. The beauty starts modestly at the junction with Interstate 15, but as the road twists and turns higher, the red walls of the Kolob finger canyons rise suddenly and spectacularly. From Kolob Canyons Viewpoint at the end of the drive, take in views of Nagunt Mesa, Shuntavi Butte, and Gregory Butte, each rising to nearly 8,000 feet in elevation. The entire round-trip drive can be completed in about an hour, without hikes. Kolob Canyons Road does sometimes close as a result of heavy snowfall. ⚠ **Storm damage closed Kolob Canyons Road beyond South Fork Picnic Area in 2023; check with the visitor center to see if it has reopened.** ✛ *Off I–15, Exit 40.*

Kolob Terrace Road
SCENIC DRIVE | Starting around 4,000 feet above the floor of Zion Canyon, and without the benefit of the canyon's breezes and shade, the landscape at the beginning of this less-traveled park road is arid—browns and grays and ambers—but not without rugged beauty. The 21-mile stretch begins 10 miles west of Springdale via the village of Virgin and winds north. As you travel along, peaks and knolls emerge from the high plateau, birds circle overhead, and you might not see more than a half-dozen cars. The drive meanders out of the park boundary and then back in again, accessing a few prominent backcountry trailheads, all the while overlooking the cliffs of North Creek. It eventually climbs into the cooler alpine wilderness, to elevations of nearly 8,000 feet.

A popular day-use trail (a $15 wilderness permit is required) leads past fossilized dinosaur tracks to The Subway, a stretch of the stream where the walls of the slot canyon close in so tightly as to form a near tunnel. Farther along the road is the Wildcat Canyon trailhead, which connects to the path overlooking North Guardian Angel. The road then leaves the park and terminates at Kolob Reservoir, beneath 8,933-foot Kolob Peak. Although paved, this narrow, twisting road is not recommended for RVs. Because of limited winter plowing, the road is closed from November or December through April or May. Although there's no fee station on this road, you are required to have paid the park entrance fee, which you can do in Springdale or at the Kolob Canyons Visitor Center. ✛ *Enter the park about 6½ miles north of Hwy. 9 in Virgin.*

Rugged and beautiful red rock landscapes await on the 21-mile Kolob Terrace Road.

SCENIC STOPS
Kolob Canyons Viewpoint
VIEWPOINT | At the end of Kolob Canyons Road, pause for a picnic and stare down the tips of the "finger" canyons to the east. Shuntavi Butte juts out from Timber Top Mountain (8,075 feet) to the southeast. Stroll the easy, 30-minute, 1-mile round-trip Timber Creek Overlook Trail, which takes in the contours of the creek and the spot where intrepid hikers go to view what is possibly the country's largest freestanding natural arch—Kolob Arch. Reaching it (via La Verkin Creek Trail) is a 14-mile round-trip undertaking, however, so hold off on it until you've consulted with the back-country ranger at the visitor center. Note that the final 2½ miles of road are closed to vehicles for road repairs until at least early 2024, but you can still access the viewpoint on foot or by bike. ⊠ *Zion National Park* ⊹ *End of Kolob Canyons Rd.*

Lava Point Overlook
VIEWPOINT | Infrequently visited, this area has a primitive camp-ground and, just beyond the park boundary, two nearby reservoirs that offer the only significant fishing opportunities near the park. Lava Point Overlook, one of the park's highest viewpoints, provides vistas of Zion Canyon from the north. The higher elevation here makes it much cooler than the Zion Canyon area. Park visitors looking for a respite from crowds and heat find the campground a nice change of pace—the six sites are available by reservation only, May through September. ⊹ *Lave Point Rd., off Kolob Terrace Rd.*

Lee Pass

VIEWPOINT | This hairpin turn on Kolob Canyons Road has a road-side pullout that provides the opportunity to glimpse deep into the canyon carved by the South Fork of Taylor Creek. This is the trailhead for the 14-mile round-trip Kolob Arch hike, which also connects you to the main section of Zion National Park via the backcountry (if overnighting in the backcountry, a wilderness permit is required). The final ½ mile of road to Lee Pass is closed to vehicles until at least early 2024, but you can still access the viewpoint on foot or by bike. ⊠ *Kolob Canyons Rd. ⚲ 3.7 miles east of Kolob Canyons Visitor Center.*

TRAILS

La Verkin Creek Trail to Kolob Arch

TRAIL | In the park's northwest corner, this 14-mile round-trip hike with an elevation gain of a little over 1,000 feet leads to one of the largest freestanding arches ever discovered. Kolob Arch spans nearly the length of a football field (287 feet) and is reached via this pleasant trail alongside La Verkin Creek and beneath the vivid red cliffs of Shuntavi Butte and Timber Top Mountain. Multiple campsites are available to make this an overnight itinerary (a wilderness permit is required for overnight stays). You can connect with the Hop Valley Trail to head into the main section of Zion National Park. *Difficult. ⚲ Trailhead: At Lee Pass, on Kolob Canyons Rd.*

The Subway Bottom-Up Trail

TRAIL | The Left Fork of North Creek is one of Zion's most awe-inspiring mapped features, although it can take some effort to find the trailhead. Determined hikers can manage its 9-mile round-trip trek from "the bottom up" in a day (plan on from 6 to 10 hours) but will need a permit. Permits are required year-round and must be applied for online; from April through October, permits are awarded by lottery. A limited number are available on last-minute notice, between seven and two days before you begin your hike.

This journey begins with a mile-long hike across the black-lava field remnants of an ancient volcanic eruption. Then you must negotiate a steep descent to the riverbed and head upstream. Highlights include intersections with several smaller canyon streams and a 30-foot trailside slab of dinosaur prints. Mostly, though, you have the pristine serenity of the river carving slick rock and then The Subway itself. You may have to climb a watery incline or two, as the river moistens the entire creek bed, but The Subway is worth the effort. Think of a subway tunnel with a river of water emanating from it instead of a train—do your research before undertaking this effort, however, as every year, hikers get lost attempting to make, and even locate, this trek. *Difficult.* ✉ *Kolob Terrace Rd., Zion National Park* ✣ *About 7 miles north of Hwy. 9 in the town of Virgin* ⊕ *www.nps.gov/zion/planyourvisit/ thesubway.htm.*

The Subway Top-Down Trail

TRAIL | Start at the Wildcat Canyon Trailhead, near Lava Point, and emerge at the Left Fork trailhead, both along Kolob Terrace Road. The 9.5-mile trek requires that you carry at least 60 feet of rope; swim through deep, debris-filled pools (wetsuits recommended); and have extensive route-finding experience. The reward is a subway tunnel–like rock formation that has been carved by the river. Descend from the arid plateau and emerge in a lush riverbed lined with trees and impossibly high cliffs. Other highlights include a 30-foot slab of dinosaur tracks, numerous side canyons, and the volcanic rock fields at the Left Fork trailhead. A permit is required and generally must be reserved well in advance (limited permits are available by lottery a week or less before a desired date and very occasionally on a walk-in basis). The trek must be completed the same day. First-timers are encouraged to travel with someone who has hiked this route to The Subway before. *Difficult.* ✉ *Wildcat Canyon Trailhead, Kolob Terrace Rd., Kolob Canyons, Zion National Park* ✣ *17 miles north of Rte. 9* ⊕ *www.nps.gov/zion/ planyourvisit/thesubway.htm.*

★ Taylor Creek Trail

TRAIL | This trail in the Kolob Canyons area descends parallel to Taylor Creek, sometimes crossing it, sometimes running along the sandstone benches that flank it. The historic Larson Cabin precedes the entrance to the canyon of the Middle Fork, where the trail becomes rougher. After the old Fife Cabin, the canyon bends to the right into Double Arch Alcove, a large, colorful grotto with a high blind arch (or arch "embryo") towering above. To Double Arch, it's 5 miles round-trip and takes about four hours. The elevation change is 450 feet. *Moderate.* ✣ *Trailhead: At Kolob Canyons Rd., about 1½ miles east of Kolob Canyons Visitor Center.*

Timber Creek Overlook Trail

TRAIL | **FAMILY** | Don't miss this short hike at the end of Kolob Canyons Road (keeping in mind that the final 2½ miles of the road are closed to vehicles—but not pedestrian or bike traffic—through at least early 2024). Covered with desert wildflowers in spring and early summer, it's barely a mile round-trip on a sandy, relatively exposed plateau above the surrounding valleys. Get a good look at the Kolob Canyons "skyline," including Shuntavi Butte in the shadow of 8,055-foot Timber Top Mountain. The last few hundred yards are a little rockier with a 100-foot ascent, but even kids and novice hikers shouldn't have any trouble with it. At the picnic area at the trailhead, you might spy lizards, chipmunks, squirrels, and the occasional long-eared, black-tailed jackrabbit. *Easy.* ✛ *Trailhead: At end of Kolob Canyons Rd.*

West Rim Trail

TRAIL | Hike from Lava Point to the Grotto (about 13½ miles) along the high plateaus west of the Virgin River. Temperatures here may be 10 to 15 degrees cooler than those in Zion Canyon due to the altitude, but your exposure to the sun may be greater, so plan accordingly. Nine campsites along the way allow you to break up this hike, and some can be reserved in advance. Permits are required year-round and applications must be made online. *Difficult.* ✉ *Kolob Terrace Rd., Zion National Park* ✛ *23 miles north of Hwy. 9 in the town of Virgin* ⊕ *www.nps.gov/zion/planyourvisit/ west-rim-trail.htm.*

VISITOR CENTERS

Kolob Canyons Visitor Center

VISITOR CENTER | Stop at this small visitor center just off Interstate 15 to pay your entrance fee and pick up books, maps, and information on exploring the Kolob Canyons section of the park. ✉ *3752 E. Kolob Canyons Rd., Exit 40 off I–15* ☎ *435/772–3256* ⊕ *www. nps.gov/zion.*

Activities

Adventure Tours

★ Zion Adventures

HIKING & WALKING | FAMILY | Since 1996, this well-respected company has guided, equipped, and offered advice on a wide range of desert adventures, including some of the top hikes in the park. Countless trekkers heading upstream on The Narrows carry Zion Adventures walking sticks and neoprene Aqua Sox footwear. The company offers special family adventures, including rock climbing and canyoneering, as well as bike tours and rentals, multiday canyoneering experiences, rock-climbing courses, photography tours, and workshops. ✉ *36 Lion Blvd.* ☎ *435/772–1001* ⊕ *www. zionadventures.com* 🎫 *From $219.*

Zion Guru

HIKING & WALKING | FAMILY | With a holistic approach to adventure, this guide service teaches canyoneering skills to beginners as young as age five and guides advanced tours as well. They offer half- and full-day rock-climbing and guided hikes, including into The Narrows, as well as yoga and wellness experiences. They also rent e-bikes and gear for The Narrows and run a shuttle service to park trailheads. ✉ *792 Zion Park Blvd.* ☎ *435/632–0462* ⊕ *www.zionguru.com* 🖃 *From $198.*

Air Tours

Zion Helicopters

AIR EXCURSIONS | This flightseeing operation 10 miles west of the park's Springdale entrance offers exhilarating helicopter rides over the park, from relatively affordable 12-minute quick zips over the canyon up to 90-minute excursions that include landing on a private red rock butte. The company also offers Bryce Canyon and Lake Powell flights. ✉ *3050 Hwy. 9, Virgin* ☎ *435/668–4185* ⊕ *www.zionhelicopters.com* 🖃 *From $99.*

Biking

The introduction of the park shuttle during the high season has improved bicycling conditions in Zion National Park; from March through November, cyclists no longer share Zion Canyon Scenic Drive with thousands of cars—though two-wheelers do need to be cautious of the large buses plying the park road throughout the day. Within the park proper, bicycles are only allowed on established park roads and on the 3½-mile Pa'rus Trail, which winds along the Virgin River in Zion Canyon. You cannot ride your bicycle through the Zion–Mt. Carmel tunnels; the only way to get your bike past this stretch of the highway is to transport it by motor vehicle.

Outside the park, southern Utah is home to a booming road cycling community. Ask at any bike shop in the region for favorite routes. Mountain bikers are increasingly drawn to Gooseberry Mesa, which locals consider equal to or better than the famous Moab slickrock mountain-biking trails.

Zion Cycles

BIKING | This shop just outside the park rents bikes by the hour or longer, sells parts, and has a full-time mechanic on duty. You can pick up trail tips and other advice from the staff here. They also offer guided road-biking treks in the park and mountain-biking excursions elsewhere in southern Utah. ✉ *868 Zion Park Blvd.* ☎ *435/772–0400* ⊕ *www.zioncycles.com* 🖃 *Guided tours from $189.*

Zion Rock & Mountain Guides

BIKING | Here you can rent Kona bikes and set up supported road-cycling trips and single-track and/or slickrock adventures at nearby Gooseberry Mesa. The company also rents car racks and trailers and can give you tips on the local trails. Day trips and multiday tours are available. Ask them about the best area trails if you prefer to explore on your own. Bike rentals start at $65 for a half-day; tour rates, which depend on group size, range from $135 per person for a half-day with five other riders to $205 for a full-day. ⊠ *1458 Zion Park Blvd., Springdale* ☎ *435/772–3303* ⊕ *www.bikingzion.com* ✉ *Guided tours from $135.*

Bird-Watching

Nearly 300 bird species call Zion Canyon home, and scores more pass through the park on their annual migrations. Some species, such as the white-throated swift and ospreys, thrive in the towering cliff walls. Red-tailed and Cooper's hawks are abundant. Closer to the ground you'll doubtless see the bold Steller's jay and scrub jay rustling around the pinyon thickets. The wild turkey population has boomed in recent years; some of the flock might come your way looking for a handout. Five species of hummingbirds reside in the park, with the black-chinned variety being the most common. You might spot members of four transient species as well. Climb to the top of Angels Landing and you might glimpse a bald eagle. Two of the park's rarest species are the Mexican spotted owl and the enormous California condor.

■TIP➔ **Ask for the Zion Bird List brochure at the visitor center or download one at** ⊕ *www.nps.gov/zion/learn/nature/birds.htm.*

Camping

The two primary campgrounds within Zion National Park are family-friendly, convenient, and generally pleasant, but in the high season they do fill up fast. Don't expect solitude as both South Campground and Watchman Campground host hundreds of campers every night in high season.

Backcountry camping in the park is an option for overnight backpackers, but make sure to get a permit at the Zion Canyon or Kolob Canyons visitor center. The primitive Lava Point Campground has no water and is generally closed from October through April. Its six sites are available by reservation.

Rates at Lava Point Campground as well as the park's two main sites are $20 per night.

Outside the park, there are options to the north, east, and west. Regardless, your best bet is to reserve ahead of time whenever possible. Private campgrounds tend to cater to families, often featuring amenities like playgrounds, showers, picnic areas, and, in some cases, swimming pools. A growing number of upscale glamping compounds provide swankier amenities.

Lava Point Campground. This little-known gem of a campground is within park limits but accessible by car only by driving the length of Kolob Terrace Road from Highway 9 in the town of Virgin, about 14 miles west of the park's South Entrance. Follow Kolob Terrace Road 20 miles north, following the signs. Your journey is rewarded with six peaceful, tree-shaded campsites at 7,890 feet above sea level (and thus about 10°F cooler on average than the Zion Park Visitor Center). These primitive campsites have firepits and picnic tables but no potable water. The adjacent trailheads offer access to the West Rim Trail and Wildcat Canyon. ⊹ *Access road off Kolob Terrace Rd.* ☎ *877/444–6777* ⊕ *www.recreation.gov* ⊋ *6 sites*

South Campground. All the sites here are under big cottonwood trees that provide some relief from the summer sun. Many of the sites are suitable for either tents or RVs, although there are no hookups. The campground operates on a reservation system and is typically open from mid-March through October. ⊹ *Hwy. 9, ½ mile north of South Entrance* ☎ *877/444–6777* ⊕ *www.recreation. gov* ⊋ *127 sites*

Watchman Campground. This large campground on the Virgin River operates year-round, with reservations available from March and November. With five loops of campsites, the campground allows everyone from tent-toting hikers to RVers to rub shoulders. Loops C and D are tent-only and quieter than the RV area. Several group sites can accommodate as many as 50 people each, turning this campground into one of the rowdier places to stay. An amphitheater hosts nightly ranger talks on topics from the park's flora and fauna to tall tales and legends. Walk to the Zion Canyon Visitor Center and to the Pa'rus Trail. Sometimes you can get same-day reservations, but don't count on it in summer. ⊹ *Access road off Zion Canyon Visitor Center parking lot* ☎ *877/444–6777* ⊕ *www. recreation.gov* ⊋ *176 sites, 95 with hookups*

Plants and Wildlife in Zion 👁

Zion, which is on the Colorado Plateau and bordered by the Great Basin and Mojave Desert provinces, has over 1,000 species of plants that thrive in environments ranging from desert to hanging garden to high plateau. Look for delicate ferns and mosses, hardy cacti, and many trees, grasses, and herbs. Poison ivy, abundant here, is one species to avoid.

When car traffic is replaced by a shuttle from March through November, wildlife returns in force. Even in high season you can spot mule deer in shady glens, especially in early morning and near dusk. You'll also see lizards and wild turkeys.

Nearly 300 species of birds reside here, from tiny hummingbirds and chickadees to eagles and pelicans. Ringtail cats (similar to raccoons) prowl the park. Evening hikes may reveal foxes, though you're more likely to spot just their tracks. Although only the rare mountain lion or black bear poses a threat, give all animals plenty of space.

Educational Programs

CLASSES AND SEMINARS
Zion National Park Forever Project
OTHER TOURS | This organization conducts in-park workshops on natural and cultural history. Topics can include edible plants, bat biology, river geology, photography, and bird-watching. Most workshops include a hike. For a glimpse of Zion's inner workings, volunteer to assist with one of their ongoing service projects. ✉ *Zion National Park* ☎ *435/772–3264* ⊕ *www.zionpark.org/events* 💲 *From $100.*

RANGER PROGRAMS
Evening Programs
NATIONAL PARK | Held each evening at 9 pm from May through October in Watchman Campground Amphitheater, these 45-minute ranger-led talks cover geology, biology, and history. You might learn about coyote calls, the night sky, the secret life of bats, or observing nature with all your senses. Slide shows and audience participation are often part of the proceedings. ✉ *Zion National Park* ⊕ *www.nps.gov/zion/planyourvisit/ranger-led-activities.htm.*

★ Expert Talks
NATIONAL PARK | Informal lectures take place on the Zion Human History Museum patio twice a day (10:30 am and 2:30 pm) and

Only 10% of visitors make it to Kolob Canyons for views like this from Timber Creek Overlook.

daily at 4 pm at Zion Lodge and may cover anything from wildlife and geology to the stories of early settlers. Talks usually last from 20 to 30 minutes, though some run longer. ✉ *Zion National Park* ⊕ *www.nps.gov/zion/planyourvisit/ranger-led-activities.htm.*

Junior Ranger Program

NATIONAL PARK | **FAMILY** | Educational activities aimed at younger visitors include the chance to earn a Junior Ranger badge. Kids do so by attending at least one nature program and completing the free *Junior Ranger Handbook,* available at visitor centers and the Zion Human History Museum. ✉ *Zion National Park* ⊕ *www.nps. gov/zion/learn/kidsyouth/beajuniorranger.htm.*

Hiking

The best way to experience Zion Canyon is to walk beneath, between, and, if you can bear it (and have good balance!), along its towering cliffs. There's something for everyone, from paved and flat river strolls to precarious cliff-side scrambles. Zion also offers a vast backcountry spanning elevations from less than 4,000 feet above sea level to as high as 8,000 feet. The wild lands encompass perilously deep canyons, forested plateaus, and broad slickrock mesas. Water is at a premium in this extreme climate, much of which can be considered unforgiving desert, and permits are required in the backcountry.

Only one of the frontcountry hikes, Angels Landing, requires a permit. Most can be accessed directly from Zion Canyon Scenic Drive; a couple are in the Kolob Canyons section of the park. You can buy detailed guides and maps for the trails at the Zion Canyon Visitor Center bookstore.

On a dry, clear day, one look at the Virgin River at the end of the Riverside Walk will demonstrate what many people figure out quite easily on their own: anyone can wade into the river upstream toward The Narrows; even better, no permit is required to travel the first 5 miles. Good hiking or wading boots are a must, and a walking stick is optional. You won't get far barefoot, and the slippery rocks can be too much for sandals. You can rent everything you need from outdoors shops in Springdale. Past the first bend, you may spend as little as 50% of the time in the water (ranging from ankle-deep to waist-deep) as there are sandbars, small beaches, and short trails along the way. Before you set out, always check weather conditions and whether there's potential for flash floods.

Whether you're heading out for a day of rock hopping or an hour of strolling, you should carry—and drink—plenty of water to counteract the effects of southern Utah's arid climate. Wear a hat, sunscreen, and sturdy shoes or boots; make sure to bring a map, and be honest with yourself about your capabilities. Getting in over your head can have serious consequences, and typically at least once a year, there's a hiking fatality in the park.

Horseback Riding

Grab your hat and boots and see Zion Canyon the way the pioneers did—on the back of a horse or mule. This is a sure way to make your trip to Zion National Park memorable. Only one outfitter is licensed to guide tours within park boundaries.

Canyon Trail Rides
HORSEBACK RIDING | **FAMILY** | Easygoing one-hour and half-day guided rides are available (minimum age 7 and 10 years, respectively). These friendly folks have been around for years and are the only outfitter for trail rides inside the park. Reservations are recommended and can be made online. The maximum weight is 220 pounds, and the season runs from March through October. ✉ *Across from Zion Lodge* ☎ *435/679–8665* ⊕ *www.canyonrides. com* 🐎 *From $50.*

Rock Climbing

The climbing in southern Utah is world-class. Keep your eyes peeled on Zion's scenic road for gear-laden climbers heading up intimidating vertical faces. Park officials recommend March through May and September through November as the best times to climb inside the park. No permit is required, except for overnight adventures.

Zion Rock & Mountain Guides

ROCK CLIMBING | FAMILY | This company takes visitors (including families with children as young as four years old) on climbing, canyoneering, cycling, and jeep routes all over southern Utah's backcountry. (Outfitters are not permitted to lead groups into Zion's legendary Narrows, Subway, or Orderville Canyon routes, although they can provide advice and equipment.) Friendly owner Dean Woods has been one of the region's eminent authorities on climbing since the 1970s. Costs depend on trip duration and group size: half-day family-climbing and standard excursions range from $135 to $240 per person, while full-day adventures cost from $205 to $500 per person, depending on how many are in your party. ⊠ *Springdale* ☎ *435/772–3303* ✉ *Guided climbs from $135.*

Chapter 4

ZION GATEWAYS

Updated by
Andrew Collins

⊙ Sights   🍴 Restaurants   🛏 Hotels   🛍 Shopping   🍸 Nightlife

★★★★☆   ★★★★☆   ★★★★☆   ★★★★☆   ★★★★☆

WELCOME TO ZION GATEWAYS

TOP REASONS TO GO

★ **Traveling through history:** Imagine life during pioneer days as you explore the historic sights of St. George.

★ **Blissing out:** Treat yourself at a luxuriant spa or partake of sophisticated dining (or both)—perhaps with views of crimson canyons.

★ **Gallery hopping:** Both Springdale and St. George abound with galleries featuring photography, paintings, and crafts that reflect the region and its aesthetic.

★ **Exploring nature:** You'll find incredible scenery for hiking and biking in and around St. George, especially at Snow Canyon State Park.

★ **Enjoying small-town charms:** Little Kanab is a scenic, friendly hub with a growing number of hip eateries and lodgings.

1 Springdale. On the southern border of Zion National Park and blessed with stunning views, this charming town of about 550 permanent residents hosts many of the park's 4.5 million annual visitors. There are plenty of wonderful places to stay and eat, as well as some great shops and galleries along the main drag.

2 Hurricane. Pronounced "HUR-ah-ken," this community on the Virgin River has experienced enormous growth, owing to the boom in nearby St. George. This is a less-expensive, less-crowded base for exploring Zion.

3 St. George. Bustling St. George offers all the services you'd expect of a city of 110,000: a regional airport, resort hotels, restaurants, a state university, and plenty of cultural activities. Situated 40 miles from Zion's entrance, it's a viable base for exploring the region.

4 Orderville. The nearest base to Zion's East Entrance, this town that also encompasses tiny unincorporated Mount Carmel Junction offers some funky small-town lodgings and scenic glamping along with the studio and museum of Maynard Dixon, one of the finest early-20th-century painters of the American West. Orderville is also handy for day trips to Bryce Canyon National Park.

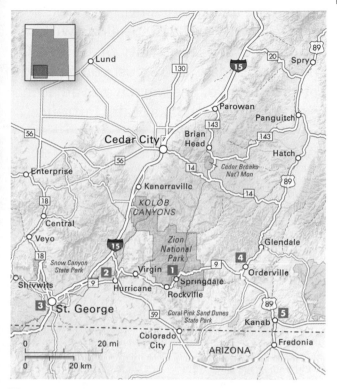

5 Kanab. Halfway between Zion and Bryce Canyon, this picturesque town surrounded by red rock cliffs and canyons makes a great base.

The region surrounding Zion National Park encompasses a few small towns—Springdale and Hurricane to the west and Orderville to the east—along with southern Utah's largest city, St. George. Of these, Springdale is the most convenient, set at the foot of the canyon and adjacent to the park's South (aka Main) Entrance.

Though inhabited by Native Americans as long ago as AD 500, Springdale got its present-day name from Mormon farmers who settled here in 1862. About 50 years later, tourism in the region began to rise with the dawn of the automobile age and the 1909 establishment of the Mukuntuweap National Monument (which became Zion National Park in 1919).

The 1930 completion of the Zion–Mt. Carmel Highway and Tunnel made the area even easier to reach. Springdale kept apace, attracting travelers with a growing number of services and amenities. Today, the town continues the legacy of putting out the welcome mat—something it does very well.

With a skyrocketing population that's fast approaching 110,000, St. George lies about 40 miles west of the park and offers several museums, an appealing mix of affordable and upscale restaurants and hotels, ample opportunities for outdoor recreation, and an airport that serves a few major Western hubs. The community was established by Mormons in the early 1860s.

The small town of Hurricane lies midway between Springdale and St. George, of which it's a growing suburb. And little Orderville is a quiet, rural town that's accessible to both Zion and Bryce. The larger regional tourism hub of Kanab lies near the Arizona border and serves as a gateway to Zion, Bryce Canyon, and the North Rim of the Grand Canyon, and it's also convenient for exploring the southern sections of Grand Staircase–Escalante National Monument as well as the Vermilion Cliffs National Monument (famous for The Wave, among other oft-photographed rock formations).

Planning

Hotels

The nearest town to Zion, small but lively Springdale has become increasingly upscale in recent years and offers a nice range of inns and hotels, ranging from casually elegant to downright luxurious—many within walking distance of the park's main visitor center. The booming city of St. George has scores of lodging options in every budget category. Hurricane is mostly the domain of budget and mid-price chain properties. And Orderville has several notable accommodations, some of them extremely close to the East Entrance of the park.

Restaurants

Almost every restaurant in the region is family-friendly and hiker-casual. Springdale and St. George offer the greatest variety, from cafés that serve breakfast all day to lively bistros where you can dine outside and enjoy spectacular views. Note that some establishments don't serve alcohol and are closed Sunday. A few also close seasonally.

⇨ *Hotel and restaurant reviews have been shortened. For full information, visit Fodors.com. Restaurant prices are the average cost of a main course at dinner, or if dinner is not served, at lunch. Hotel prices are the lowest cost of a standard double room in high season.*

What It Costs			
$	$$	$$$	$$$$
RESTAURANTS			
under $20	$20–$30	$31–$40	over $40
HOTELS			
under $200	$200–$350	$351–$500	over $500

Springdale

Adjacent to the South Entrance of Zion National Park.

This gorgeously situated town of about 550 has nearly doubled in population since 1990, thanks in large part to its bordering Zion

National Park. While you will find an array of hotels, restaurants, and shops here, Springdale still retains its small-town charm.

GETTING HERE AND AROUND

Unless you take a shuttle bus from St. George or Las Vegas, you'll need a car to get to Springdale, which is bisected by Highway 9, but getting around once you're here is easy. The complimentary Springdale Line shuttle bus runs from March through November, making it easy to travel through town and to Zion National Park, where you can connect to the free Zion Canyon shuttle. It's also a pleasant town to stroll through, with nearly all businesses situated along the main thoroughfare. In winter, when there are fewer crowds, a car is handy for getting around town and into the park.

Sights

Grafton

GHOST TOWN | FAMILY | A stone school, a dusty cemetery, and a few wooden structures are all that remain of the nearby town of Grafton, which is between Springdale and Hurricane, a few miles west of the turnoff onto Bridge Road in Rockville. This ghost town, which has a dramatic setting with striking views of Zion's peaks, has been featured in several films, including *Butch Cassidy and the Sundance Kid.* ⊠ *End of W. Grafton Rd., Springdale.*

🍴 Restaurants

The Bit & Spur

$$ | SOUTHWESTERN | This laid-back Springdale institution has been delighting locals and tourists since the late 1980s, offering a well-rounded menu that includes fresh fish and pasta dishes, but the emphasis is on creative Southwestern fare, such as roasted-sweet-potato-and-pork tamales and chili-rubbed rib-eye steak. Craft beers and the popular house-made sangria complement the zesty cuisine. **Known for:** lighter Mexican fare in the Backyard Taco Shack & Cantina; live music; outdoor dining by a fountain beneath shade trees. ⑤ *Average main: $22* ⊠ *1212 Zion Park Blvd., Springdale* ☎ *435/772–3498* ⊕ *www.bitandspur.com* ☺ *No lunch. Closed Mon.–Thurs. in Dec. and Jan.*

★ King's Landing Bistro

$$ | MODERN AMERICAN | Ask to be seated on the patio—with dramatic views of the area's red rock monoliths—when dining at this casually stylish bistro at the popular Driftwood Lodge. The artfully presented cuisine tends toward creative American with Mediterranean influences—think king salmon with saffron couscous, fettuccine Bolognese with black truffle oil, and charred Spanish

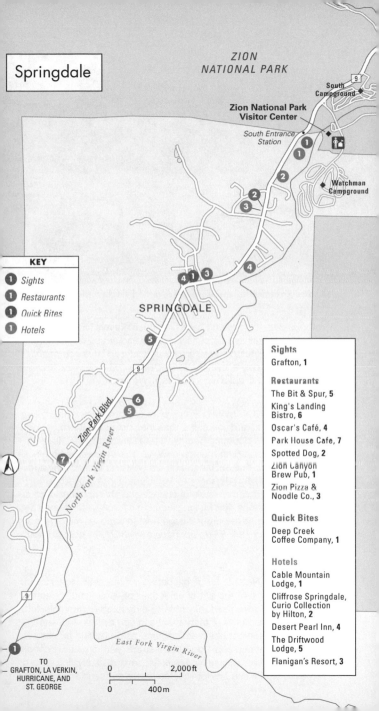

Springdale

ZION NATIONAL PARK

South Campground

Zion National Park Visitor Center

South Entrance Station

Watchman Campground

SPRINGDALE

Zion Park Blvd.

North Fork Virgin River

East Fork Virgin River

TO GRAFTON, LA VERKIN, HURRICANE, AND ST. GEORGE

KEY

- ● Sights
- ● Restaurants
- ● Quick Bites
- ● Hotels

Sights
Grafton, 1

Restaurants
The Bit & Spur, 5
King's Landing Bistro, 6
Oscar's Café, 4
Park House Cafe, 7
Spotted Dog, 2
Zion Canyon Brew Pub, 1
Zion Pizza & Noodle Co., 3

Quick Bites
Deep Creek Coffee Company, 1

Hotels
Cable Mountain Lodge, 1
Cliffrose Springdale, Curio Collection by Hilton, 2
Desert Pearl Inn, 4
The Driftwood Lodge, 5
Flanigan's Resort, 3

0   2,000ft
0   400m

A collection of tombstones makes a fine epitaph for the ghost town of Grafton.

octopus with chorizo and baba ghanoush. **Known for:** interesting artisanal cocktail list; emphasis on local and seasonal produce; rich desserts, including seasonal fruit crisps. $ *Average main: $29* ⊠ *1515 Zion Park Blvd., Springdale* ☎ *435/772–7422* ⊕ *www. klbzion.com* ☾ *Closed Sun. and Mon. No lunch.*

Oscar's Café

$ | **SOUTHWESTERN** | **FAMILY** | Prepare for an active day with a filling breakfast, or reward yourself after a long hike with lunch or dinner at this welcoming Southwestern café with a big, inviting patio offering stunning mountain views. The pork *verde* breakfast burrito and huevos rancheros are hearty and delicious, and excellent lunch and dinner options include flame-broiled garlic burgers topped with provolone cheese and shrimp tacos with a creamy lime sauce. **Known for:** blue-corn nachos with cheese and guacamole; creative burgers; large heated patio. $ *Average main: $19* ⊠ *948 Zion Park Blvd., Springdale* ☎ *435/772–3232* ⊕ *www. oscarscafe.com.*

Park House Cafe

$ | **AMERICAN** | Notable for its big patio with fantastic views into the park and for one of the better selections of vegan and vegetarian dishes in town, this funky little café decorated with colorful artwork serves plenty of tasty meat and egg dishes, too. The grilled ham Benedict has plenty of fans, as do buffalo burgers with Havarti cheese and apple-pear-berry salads with organic greens, feta, and walnuts. **Known for:** breakfast served all day; full slate of espresso drinks and smoothies; ice cream sundaes and banana

splits. $ *Average main: $15* ⊠ *1880 Zion Park Blvd., Springdale*
☎ *435/772–0100* ⊘ *No dinner.*

Spotted Dog

$$ | MODERN AMERICAN | At this upscale, light-filled restaurant with
an eclectic menu that's rich on fresh pastas and creative meat and
seafood dishes, the staff make you feel right at home even if you
saunter in wearing hiking shoes. The exposed wood beams and
large windows that frame the surrounding trees and rock cliffs set
a Western mood, with tablecloths and original artwork supplying a
dash of refinement. **Known for:** interesting but accessible wine list;
lovely patio for alfresco dining; much of the produce is grown on
site. $ *Average main: $24* ⊠ *Flanigan's Inn, 428 Zion Park Blvd.,
Springdale* ☎ *435/772–0700* ⊕ *flanigans.com/dine* ⊘ *No lunch.*

★ Zion Canyon Brew Pub

$$ | AMERICAN | Relax after a rugged day of hiking with a flight of
ales or a juicy elk burger in the beer garden of southern Utah's oldest craft beer maker, Zion Brewery, which is just steps from the
park's South Entrance. The kitchen turns out excellent pub grub,
such as stout-glazed buffalo meat loaf and beer-battered fish-and-
chips, and there's live music most weekend evenings. **Known
for:** serves food later than most places in town; excellent craft
beers; lovely setting overlooking the Virgin River. $ *Average main:
$20* ⊠ *95 Zion Park Blvd., Springdale* ☎ *435/772–0336* ⊕ *www.
zionbrewery.com/the-brew-pub.*

Zion Pizza & Noodle Co.

$ | ITALIAN | FAMILY | Creative pizzas and a kicked back atmosphere
in a former church make this a great place to replenish after a
trek through the canyon. Meat lovers appreciate the Cholesterol
Hiker pizza, topped with pepperoni, Canadian bacon, and Italian
sausage, but the Thai chicken and rosemary-garlic pies are also
delicious. **Known for:** stone-slate pizzas with creative toppings;
attractive garden seating; good craft beer list. $ *Average main:
$18* ⊠ *868 Zion Park Blvd., Springdale* ☎ *435/772–3815* ⊕ *www.
zionpizzanoodle.com* ⊘ *No lunch. Closed Dec.–Feb.*

☕ Coffee and Quick Bites

★ Deep Creek Coffee Company

$ | CAFÉ | Stop by this cheerful coffeehouse with hanging plants
and several tables on a spacious side patio to fuel up before your
big park adventure or to grab some healthy sustenance for later.
Hearty cacao-acai and chipotle aioli–quinoa bowls, toast with
goat cheese and fresh strawberries, bagels with the requisite
schmears, breakfast burritos, and house-made granola are among

the tasty offerings. **Known for:** opens at 6 am daily; potent house-made cold brew; delicious smoothies. $ *Average main: $10* ⊠ *932 Zion Park Blvd., Springdale* ☎ *435/669–8849* ⊕ *www.deepcreek-coffee.com* ☾ *No dinner.*

🛏 Hotels

★ Cable Mountain Lodge

$$ | HOTEL | This contemporary lodge with a large swimming pool and a serene full-service spa is the closest hotel in Springdale to Zion—it's a scenic five-minute walk over a footbridge across the Virgin River. **Pros:** steps from Zion National Park's South Entrance; many suites have full kitchens; beautiful picnic area along river with gas grills and tables. **Cons:** no breakfast (but a coffeehouse and market steps away); not all rooms have park views; sometimes books up weeks in advance. $ *Rooms from: $289* ⊠ *147 Zion Park Blvd., Springdale* ☎ *435/772–3366, 877/712–3366* ⊕ *www.cablemountainlodge.com* ⇋ *52 rooms* ❑ *No Meals.*

Cliffrose Springdale, Curio Collection by Hilton

$$$ | HOTEL | The canyon views, acres of lush lawns and flowers, and pool and two-tier waterfall hot tubs at this stylish riverside hotel make it more than a place to rest your head, and you could throw a rock across the river and hit Zion National Park. **Pros:** close to Zion's South Entrance; enchanting grounds and views; excellent restaurant and full-service spa. **Cons:** steep rates; lots of foot and car traffic nearby; no elevator. $ *Rooms from: $368* ⊠ *281 Zion Park Blvd., Springdale* ☎ *435/772–3234* ⊕ *www.cliffroselodge. com* ⇋ *53 rooms* ❑ *No Meals.*

★ Desert Pearl Inn

$$$ | HOTEL | Offering rooms of 650 square feet or larger with vaulted ceilings, oversize windows, sitting areas, small kitchens with wet bars and dishwashers, and pleasing contemporary decor, this riverside lodge is special. **Pros:** spacious, smartly designed rooms; excellent Camp Outpost Co. restaurant next door; rooms facing river have balconies or terraces. **Cons:** often books up well in advance; breakfast not included; pets not permitted. $ *Rooms from: $379* ⊠ *707 Zion Park Blvd., Springdale* ☎ *435/772–8888, 888/828–0898* ⊕ *www.desertpearl.com* ⇋ *72 rooms* ❑ *No Meals.*

The Driftwood Lodge

$$ | HOTEL | The bright and contemporary rooms at this friendly, mid-priced roadside lodge have balconies or patios and great views of the Virgin River and surrounding canyons, along with refrigerators and large flat-screen TVs. **Pros:** many rooms overlook the river and park; superb restaurant; attractive pool and picnic area. **Cons:** least expensive rooms have limited view or balcony; breakfast not included; limited pet reservations must be booked by phone. Ⓢ *Rooms from: $239* ✉ *1515 Zion Park Blvd., Springdale* ☏ *435/772–3262* ⊕ *www.driftwoodlodge.net* ➩ *63 rooms* ⦿l *No Meals.*

Flanigan's Resort

$$ | HOTEL | A tranquil, nicely landscaped inn with canyon views and a small pool, Flanigan's offers spacious, elegantly appointed accommodations, including two private villas and suites that sleep six; some units have a patio or a deck. **Pros:** easy shuttle ride or pleasant walk to Zion Canyon Visitor Center; a meditation maze on the hilltop; one of the better restaurants in town. **Cons:** not all rooms have views; smaller property that tends to book up quickly; breakfast isn't complimentary (and isn't available in winter). Ⓢ *Rooms from: $249* ✉ *450 Zion Park Blvd., Springdale* ☏ *435/772–3244* ⊕ *www.flanigans.com* ➩ *32 rooms* ⦿l *No Meals.*

🛍 Shopping

David J. West Gallery

ART GALLERIES | The radiant photography of artist David J. West captures Zion's natural setting in its full grandeur, along with Bryce, Cedar Breaks, Arches, and other stunning spots throughout Utah and the Southwest. The gallery also stocks contemporary landscape paintings and geologically inspired pottery. ✉ *801 Zion Park Blvd., Springdale* ☏ *435/772–3510* ⊕ *www.davidjwest.com.*

★ Worthington Gallery

ART GALLERIES | The emphasis at this superb gallery in a circa-1880s pioneer home is on regional art, including pottery, works in glass, jewelry, beguiling copper wind sculptures by Lyman Whitaker, and paintings by more than a dozen artists that capture the dramatic beauty of southern Utah. ✉ *789 Zion Park Blvd., Springdale* ☏ *435/772–3446* ⊕ *www.worthingtongallery.com.*

Hurricane

22 miles west of Zion National Park's South Entrance.

Midway between Zion and St. George, this small but steadily growing high-desert town—along with the smaller village of Virgin to the east—is becoming an increasingly popular base for exploring the park and surrounding region, especially as new hotels and restaurants continue to open. Nearby Gooseberry Mesa is one of the best places for mountain biking in Utah.

In-the-know mountain bikers head to Gooseberry Mesa near the town of Hurricane.

GETTING HERE AND AROUND

From St. George, take I–5 north and then Highway 9 east. A car is a must for exploring this area.

🍽 Restaurants

Main Street Cafe

$ | AMERICAN | This colorful storefront eatery in historic downtown Hurricane pours one of the region's best cups of coffee, a fine prelude or follow-up to the salads, sandwiches, hearty omelets, homemade soups, flavorful pastas, and generous hamburgers on the menu. If you have the time, linger outside on the shaded patio and watch the hummingbirds. **Known for:** handy location for trips east toward Zion National Park; pretty outdoor seating area; big portions. ⑤ *Average main: $15* ⌂ *138 S. Main St., Hurricane* ☎ *435/635–9080* ⊕ *www.mainstreetcafehurricane.com* ⊗ *Closed Sun.*

★ Peruvian Flavors

$ | PERUVIAN | What you could easily mistake for a classic diner with its black-and-white-checkered floor and green-vinyl seats is actually one of the few restaurants in the state specializing in the boldly flavored cuisine of the Andes. At this friendly café across from downtown Hurricane's civic park, enjoy classics like grilled rotisserie chicken with Peruvian spices and chilies, Venezuelan arepas stuffed with shredded beef, and fried rice with seasoned ham, eggs, and vegetables. **Known for:** cheerful setting and staff;

arroz con leche; shrimp-and-fish ceviche. ⑤ *Average main: $11* ✉ *68 W. State St., Hurricane* ☎ *435/703–6216* ⊕ *www.facebook. com/flavorsperuvian* ⊗ *Closed Sun. No lunch Tues.*

🛏 Hotels

Fairfield Inn & Suites Virgin Zion National Park

$ | **HOTEL** | **FAMILY** | The largest hotel in southern Utah may be a pretty conventional mid-range chain property, but it also offers some appealing perks, including large and separate kid and adult pools, expansive canyon vistas, and significantly cheaper rates than hotels in Springdale, which is less than a 20-minute drive. **Pros:** quiet setting; equidistant to Springdale and St. George; nice views of Zion's Kolob Canyons. **Cons:** pleasant but perfunctory room decor; no dining within walking distance; some rooms overlook the road. ⑤ *Rooms from: $149* ✉ *1 Camino del Rio* ☎ *435/635–9758* ⊕ *www.marriott.com* ➼ *190 rooms* ⑩ *Free Breakfast.*

Under Canvas Zion

$$$ | **RESORT** | This high-end, Insta-worthy glamping compound enjoys an eye-popping setting just west of the minimally trafficked Kolob Terrace Entrance to Zion National Park. **Pros:** downright plush bedding and furnishings; far from the crowds of Springdale and Zion Canyon; incredible Zion-adjacent setting. **Cons:** a half-hour drive from Springdale and Zion's South Entrance; spendy for tent accommodations (however gorgeously appointed) with no Wi-Fi or electricity; can be uncomfortably hot in summer. ⑤ *Rooms from: $369* ✉ *3955 Kolob Terrace Rd., Hurricane* ☎ *888/496–1148* ⊕ *www.undercanvas.com/camps/zion* ⊗ *Closed early Nov.–early Mar.* ➼ *48 units* ⑩ *No Meals.*

🏃 Activities

BIKING
Gooseberry Mesa

BIKING | The more than 18 miles of mountain-biking trails on this mesa near Hurricane aren't well traveled, which is good news and bad news. On the plus side, there aren't hordes of fat-tire fanatics to spoil your view of the pristine desert wilderness. However, the trails themselves, through gulches and canyons and across slickrock, can be a little hard to follow. At most of the difficult (and unnervingly steep) spots along this tortuous path, there are easier alternatives if you lose your nerve. Come here for solitary and technical single-track challenges, and be aware that the unpaved roads to the trailheads can be impassable after heavy rains. ⚓ *Off Hwy. 59* ☎ *435/688–3200* ⊕ *www.blm.gov/visit/ gooseberry-mesa-national-recreation-trail.*

Over the Edge Sports

BIKING | This well-stocked shop in downtown Hurricane has an extensive selection of mountain bikes as well as e-bikes for rent. The knowledgeable staff can tell you everything you need to know about tackling the trails of Gooseberry Mesa as well as countless other biking venues in southern Utah. ✉ *76 E. 100 S* ☎ *435/635– 5455* ⊕ *otesports.com/locations/hurricane* 🖃 *From $49 per day.*

St. George

45 miles west of Zion National Park's South Entrance, and 18 miles west of Hurricane.

Believing the mild year-round climate ideal for growing cotton, Brigham Young dispatched 309 Latter-day Saints families in 1861 to found St. George. They were to raise cotton and silkworms and to establish a textile industry, to make up for textile shortages resulting from the Civil War.

Flash forward to the early 2020s, and St. George is the fastest-growing metropolitan area in the country—the city population has soared from about 11,500 to nearly 110,000 over the past four decades. It's the cultural and recreational hub of southern Utah, a favorite place to relocate for both retirees (who appreciate the warm winters) and younger families and entrepreneurs (lured by the high quality of life, stunning scenery, and growing number of restaurants, shops, and other services). It's a popular destination (and base for nearby Zion National Park) year-round, but fall through spring is especially appealing and free of summer's sometimes oppressive heat. One very popular draw is the **Dixie Roundup** (⊕ *www.stgeorgelions.com*), a three-day rodeo held every mid-September since the 1930s.

Although the metro area sprawls in all directions, except where soaring red rock hills (mostly to the north) prevent expansion, St. George has an attractive, pedestrian-friendly downtown anchored by a stately white stucco–clad Mormon temple that dates to 1877. Other appealing areas include historic Santa Clara, a small village several miles west of downtown with a cluster of well-preserved pioneer homes, and the town of Ivins, which is home to the Sedona-esque Kayenta Art Village and is also the gateway for exploring gorgeous Snow Canyon State Park.

GETTING HERE AND AROUND

This fast-growing, sprawling city is bisected by Interstate 15, and although the very heart of downtown is pedestrian-friendly, you need a car to explore outlying areas. It is possible to get from St. George to Zion National Park via the St. George Shuttle, which has scheduled service a few times per day.

◉ Sights

Brigham Young Winter Home and Office

HISTORIC HOME | Mormon leader Brigham Young spent the last seven winters of his life in the warm, sunny climate of St. George. Built of adobe on a sandstone-and-basalt foundation and now a museum, this two-story home, with pretty green and red trim and well-tended gardens, contains a portrait of Young over one fireplace and furnishings from the late 19th century. Visits are by guided tour. ⊠ 67 W. 200 N, St. George ☎ 435/673–2517 ⊕ history.churchofjesuschrist.org/landing/historic-sites ⊠ Free.

★ Kayenta Art Village

ARTS CENTER | In the heart of an upscale, contemporary planned community in Ivins, not far from Tuacahn Center for the Arts and Snow Canyon State Park, this beautifully situated arts colony contains several of southern Utah's top galleries, including Gallery 873, known for jewelry and ceramics; Kayenta Desert Arboretum & Desert Rose Labyrinth and Sculpture Gardens, which visitors can freely stroll through; Zia Pottery Studio, a co-op operated by talented local potters; and several others. Set against a red rock landscape, it's an enchanting neighborhood to stroll through, especially during the Art in Kayenta outdoor festival in mid-October. Also check to see what's on at the Center for the Arts at Kayenta—which presents lectures, movies, theater, and concerts—or grab a bite at the excellent Xetava Café or the expansion Xetava Bar & Kitchen, which opened in 2023. ⊠ 875 Coyote Gulch Ct., Ivins ☎ 435/674–2306 ⊕ www.kayentaartvillage.com.

★ Red Hills Desert Garden

GARDEN | Opened in 2015 as the state's first botanic garden devoted to desert conservation, this beautiful space in the red hills on downtown's northern edge is ideal for a peaceful stroll and learning about water-efficient plants. More than 5,000 of them—including fragrant mesquite trees, prickly pear cactus, blue agave, Joshua trees, weeping yucca, and desert willows—thrive here, along with a meandering stream that's stocked with desert suckers, Virgin River chub, and other native species. Paths also lead past a number of boulders that preserve the tracks of dinosaurs that roamed here some 200 million years ago. The garden adjoins

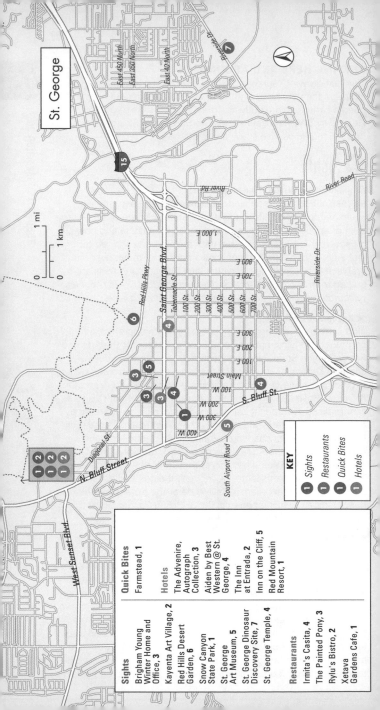

St. George

KEY
- 1 Sights
- 1 Restaurants
- 1 Quick Bites
- 1 Hotels

Sights

Brigham Young Winter Home and Office, 3

Kayenta Art Village, 2

Red Hills Desert Garden, 6

Snow Canyon State Park, 1

St. George Art Museum, 5

St. George Dinosaur Discovery Site, 7

St. George Temple, 4

Restaurants

Irmita's Casita, 4

The Painted Pony, 3

Rylu's Bistro, 2

Xetava Gardens Cafe, 1

Quick Bites

Farmstead, 1

Hotels

The Advenire, Autograph Collection, 3

Aiden by Best Western @ St. George, 4

The Inn at Entrada, 2

Inn on the Cliff, 5

Red Mountain Resort, 1

rugged Pioneer Park, a 52-acre expanse of rock-climbing and hiking terrain, with barbecue pits, picnic pavilions and tables, and both short and long trails. ⊠ *375 E. Red Hills Pkwy., St. George* ☎ *435/673–3617* ⊕ *www.redhillsdesertgarden.com.*

★ Snow Canyon State Park

STATE/PROVINCIAL PARK | **FAMILY** | Named not for winter weather but after a pair of pioneering Utahans named Snow, this breathtaking 7,400-acre red rock wonderland—about 10 miles northwest of St. George and located entirely within Red Cliffs Desert Reserve—abounds with natural wonders, many of which are easily explored from the well-marked parking areas. The best strategy is to enter from the south from Ivins and drive north along the 4½-mile park road to Highway 18, which leads south back to St. George.

Nearly 40 miles of hiking trails lead to lava cones, petrified dunes, cactus gardens, and high-contrast vistas. Great options if you have only a couple of hours include the short trek to the soaring slot canyon known as Jenny's Canyon and the slightly longer (it takes an hour) Lava Tube Trail. Upper Galoot is a pretty picnic area with grills as well as a short trail lined with interesting interpretative signs about the desert tortoise. From the campground you can scramble up huge sandstone mounds and look across the entire valley. Park staff lead occasional guided hikes. ⊠ *1002 Snow Canyon Dr., St. George* ☎ *435/628–2255* ⊕ *stateparks.utah.gov/parks/snow-canyon* ⊠ *$15 per vehicle.*

St. George Art Museum

ART MUSEUM | **FAMILY** | The downtown centerpiece of St. George's growing art scene occupies an attractively reimagined former sugar-beet warehouse. The permanent collection celebrates the works of mostly regionally based potters, photographers, and painters, many of them depicting the region's spectacular landscapes. Rotating exhibits highlight local history and lore and showcase emerging contemporary talents. There's also a Family Discovery Center, with materials for kids to create their own works. ⊠ *47 E. 200 N, St. George* ☎ *435/627–4525* ⊕ *www.sgcity.org/artmuseum* ⊠ *$15 suggested donation* ☺ *Closed Sun. and Mon.*

St. George Dinosaur Discovery Site

SCIENCE MUSEUM | **FAMILY** | Unearthed in 2000 by property developers, this site preserves and exhibits ancient footprints left by dinosaurs from the Jurassic Period millions of years ago. A modern museum displays dinosaur fossils and replicas and presents several short informative videos about the Jurassic era. There's an interactive area for children and a Dino Park outside the museum with shaded picnic tables and a "Walk Through Time" exhibit.

✉ *2180 E. Riverside Dr., St. George* ☎ *435/574–3466* ⊕ *www.utahdinosaurs.org* 🎟 *$10* 🕐 *Closed Tues.*

St. George Temple

CHURCH | The red-sandstone temple, plastered over with white stucco, was completed in 1877 and was the first Mormon temple in southwest Utah. It has served as a meeting place for both Mormons and other congregations over the decades. Today, only members of the Church of Jesus Christ of Latter-day Saints can enter the temple, but a visitor center next door offers guided tours of the visitor center and grounds. The temple reopened in late 2023 after being closed for several years of renovations that have made it more accessible and energy-efficient and restored the exterior and interior to better replicate the original temple. ✉ *250 E. 400 S, St. George* ☎ *435/673–5181* ⊕ *www.churchofjesus-christ.org/landing/historic-sites.*

🍴 Restaurants

Irmita's Casita

$ | **MEXICAN** | **FAMILY** | A reliable standby for tasty Mexican-American fare since 1993, this humble spot serves affordable, no-nonsense food that can be quite spicy if requested. Specialties include pork tortas, massive burritos smothered in red or green sauce, and shrimp enchiladas. **Known for:** steak chilaquiles at breakfast; chicken mole poblano; Mexican soft drinks and juices. ⑤ *Average main: $12* ✉ *95 W. 700 S* ☎ *435/703–9162* ⊕ *irmitas-casita.business.site* 🚫 *No credit cards* 🕐 *Closed Sun. and Mon.*

★ The Painted Pony

$$$ | **MODERN AMERICAN** | A charming patio overlooking Ancestor Square with contemporary Southwestern art on the walls provides a romantic setting for enjoying contemporary American fare with an emphasis on seasonal ingredients, many from the owners' private organic garden. Consider chorizo-stuffed quail with a tamarind glaze, followed by a juniper-brined bone-in pork chop with stuffed pears and smoked-tomato relish, and don't pass up the standout sides that include chipotle bread pudding, zucchini fritters, and blue cheese–walnut–stuffed pears. **Known for:** knowledgeable servers; one of the best wine lists in town; seasonally changing bread pudding. ⑤ *Average main: $37* ✉ *2 W. St. George Blvd., St. George* ☎ *435/634–1700* ⊕ *www.painted-pony.com* 🕐 *No lunch Sun.*

★ Rylu's Bistro

$$ | **CONTEMPORARY** | In a handsomely restored little house in the tree-lined, historic village of Santa Clara—about 15 minutes west of downtown St. George—this sweet, cozy neighborhood restaurant with seating in a colorful front garden serves extraordinarily tasty, locally sourced contemporary American–Mediterranean fare. It's worth the trip to this slightly off-the-beaten-path locale to savor coconut *labneh* with spicy harissa, charred heirloom tomatoes, and hazelnut dukkah and seared skirt steak with jalapeño-parsley *chermoula*. **Known for:** exceptional farm-to-table cuisine; charming, historic setting; thoughtful wine list (and inexpensive corkage fee if you bring your own bottle). ⑤ *Average main: $29 ⊠ 2862 Santa Clara Dr.* ☎ *435/414–7509* ⊕ *www.rylusbistro.com* ✆ *Closed Sun. and Mon. No lunch.*

★ Xetava Gardens Café

$$ | **MODERN AMERICAN** | This beautifully designed adobe oasis in the Kayenta Art Village in Ivins, about 10 miles northwest of St. George, offers gracious indoor and outdoor seating, the latter overlooking fragrant high-desert gardens and the surrounding red rock ramparts. Pronounced *zay-tah-vah*, the space began as a coffee bar and is still a source of lattes and mochas, but you'll also find an eclectic selection of globally inspired all-day fare, including blue-corn waffles, ham ciabattas, peach-glazed organic chicken, and wild mushroom burgers. **Known for:** steps from several art galleries; well-curated beer, wine, and cocktail list; croissant bread pudding with caramel sauce. ⑤ *Average main: $21 ⊠ 815 Coyote Gulch Ct.* ☎ *435/656–0166* ⊕ *www.xetava.com* ✆ *Closed Tues. and Wed. No dinner Mon.*

🍵 Coffee and Quick Bites

★ Farmstead

$ | **BAKERY** | This hip sidewalk café and bakery on the ground floor of a downtown St. George apartment building is a pleasing option for both decadent sweets—think passionfruit-coconut–glazed doughnuts and blood-orange tarts—and filling sandwiches on crusty house-baked breads. Notable drink options include brown sugar–cinnamon lattes and high-octane cold brews. **Known for:** sensational doughnuts and pastries; shaded sidewalk seating; hearty sandwiches and pizzas. ⑤ *Average main: $9 ⊠ 18 S. 200 W, St. George* ☎ *435/986–7777* ⊕ *www.farmsteadbakery.com* ✆ *Closed Mon. and Tues. No dinner.*

🛏 Hotels

★ The Advenire, Autograph Collection

$$ | **HOTEL** | A strikingly contemporary, upscale hotel that's directly across the street from the buzzy shopping and dining of Ancestor

Square, this stylish member of Marriott Bonvoy's indie-spirited Autograph Collection exudes hipness with its hardwood floors, bold-print pillows and chairs, high-tech entertainment centers, and cushy bedding. **Pros:** stylish, cosmopolitan decor; superb on-site restaurant; steps from downtown dining and retail. **Cons:** neighborhood can be crowded and noisy; steep pet fee; parking is valet only ($18) unless you find a spot on the street. $ Rooms from: $215 ⊠ 25 W. St. George Blvd., St. George ☎ 435/522–5022 ⊕ www.theadvenirehotel.com ⇆ 60 rooms ❖ No Meals.

Aiden by Best Western @ St. George

$ | **MOTEL** | **FAMILY** | Within walking distance of downtown, this retro-inspired member of Best Western's stylish Aiden boutique hotel brand is a great value with an attractive pool, hot tub, and sun deck, and rates include a full breakfast buffet and free bike rentals. **Pros:** cool mid-century modern design; soda–ice cream float bar that's a hit with kids; central location. **Cons:** no gym; on a busy road; rooms set around a parking lot. $ Rooms from: $115 ⊠ 316 E. St. George Blvd., St. George ☎ 435/673–3541 ⊕ www. aidenstg.com ⇆ 30 rooms ❖ Free Breakfast.

The Inn at Entrada

$$ | **RESORT** | Hikers, spagoers, and—above all—golfers flock to this plush boutique resort set amid the red rock canyons northwest of downtown, surrounded by a world-class Johnny Miller–designed golf course that was completely rebuilt in 2022 and offering a top-notch spa, pool, and fitness facility. **Pros:** adjoins one of the top golf courses in the state; attractive Southwest-inspired contemporary decor; terrific spa. **Cons:** 10- to 15-minute drive from downtown dining; bathrooms are a little dark; can get very expensive depending on time of year. $ Rooms from: $280 ⊠ 2588 W. Sinagua Trail ☎ 435/634–7100 ⊕ www.innatentrada.com ⇆ 57 rooms ❖ No Meals.

★ Inn on the Cliff

$ | **HOTEL** | It's all about the panoramic views at this exceptionally well-maintained mid-century modern boutique hotel set high on a ridge overlooking downtown St. George and the red rocks beyond. **Pros:** reasonable rates for such a nice property; stunning views; continental breakfast delivered to your room. **Cons:** no pets; not within walking distance of downtown; restaurant closed on Sunday. $ Rooms from: $199 ⊠ 511 S. Tech Ridge Dr., St. George ☎ 435/216–5864 ⊕ www.innonthecliff.com ⇆ 27 rooms ❖ Free Breakfast.

★ Red Mountain Resort

$ | **RESORT** | This luxurious red rock hideaway, with its stunning surroundings near the mouth of Snow Canyon, offers a range of

Petrified sand dunes are among the red rock formations in Snow Canyon State Park.

outdoor adventures and fitness and wellness options, from fitness classes, hikes, and yoga sessions to red clay–lavender body wraps and warm Himalayan salt stone massages. **Pros:** world-class spa and fitness facilities; handsome contemporary design fits in with natural surroundings; a range of meal, spa, and activity packages available. **Cons:** caters more to activity-seekers than those looking to relax; 15-minute drive northwest of St. George; all those potential treatment, activity, and meal add-ons can get pricey. *Rooms from: $189* *1275 E. Red Mountain Circle, Ivins* *435/673–4905, 877/246–4453* *www.redmountainresort.com* *106 units* *No Meals.*

Performing Arts

★ Tuacahn Center for the Arts

CONCERTS | At this magnificent outdoor amphitheater nestled in a natural red-sandstone cove, you can watch touring Broadway musicals and concerts by noted pop artists. *1100 Tuacahn Dr.* *800/746–9882 box office* *www.tuacahn.org.*

Activities

BIKING

Cyclists from all over the world are drawn to St. George's 60-plus miles of paved bike trails, which meander past the black lava flows and red rocks of Snow Canyon State Park and connect with a half-dozen other parks around the city. Mountain bikers should check out the interconnected 6-mile Prospector–Church Rocks Trail in nearby Washington—it also boasts mesmerizing red rock views.

Visit ⊕ *trails.greaterzion.com* for an interactive map.

Bicycles Unlimited

BIKING | A trusted southern Utah biking resource, this shop rents mountain and road bikes and also offers maps and advice about great rides in the area. ⊠ *90 S. 100 E, St. George* ☎ *435/673–4492* ⊕ *www.bicyclesunlimited.com* ⊠ *Rentals from $65 for a half-day.*

Orderville

18 miles east of Zion National Park's East Entrance.

This easygoing farming town of 600, along with the neighboring unincorporated communities of Mount Carmel and Mount Carmel Junction, lies at the southern end of the picturesque U.S. 89 corridor, about a 20-minute drive from both Zion National Park's East Entrance and the many restaurants and shops of Kanab. Services here are a bit limited, but a handful of lodgings and eateries serve the growing number of visitors who appreciate the convenience for Zion and Bryce Canyon, minus the crowds. Don't miss the studio of Maynard Dixon, who was rightly considered one of the finest painters of the American West. And if you're here in early August, you can attend the festive and family-friendly Kane County Fair.

GETTING HERE AND AROUND

Tiny Orderville and even smaller Mount Carmel Junction are along U.S. 89, between Kanab (about 20 miles south) and Panguitch (about 45 miles north). A car is a must in these parts.

◉ Sights

Maynard Dixon and Edith Hamlin Home and Studio

ART MUSEUM | Midway between Orderville and Mount Carmel Junction, you can tour the final summer residence of the famous painter of Western life and landscapes. Dixon lived from 1875 to 1946 and was married to the renowned WPA photographer Dorothea Lange, and, following their divorce, to San Francisco muralist Edith Hamlin. He and Hamlin summered on this property from 1939 until his death; shortly after, she scattered his ashes on a ridge behind the property, which consists of the original log cabin structure and an exceptional Western Art gallery, both of which are maintained by the nonprofit Thunderbird Foundation for the

Arts. From March through November, self-guided and docent-led tours (by appointment only) are offered. The gallery and gift shop are open daily year-round. ⊠ 2200 S. State St., (U.S. 89), Mount Carmel ☎ 435/648–2653 ⊕ www.thunderbirdfoundation.com 🔁 Gallery free, self-guided tours $20, guided tours $40 ⊗ Closed Sun. and Mon.

🍴 Restaurants

Cordwood

$$ | **MODERN AMERICAN** | Edison bulbs, timber walls, local landscape photos, and actual stacked cords of wood impart a rustic-elegant ambience at this casually upscale restaurant just 4 miles beyond Zion National Park's East Entrance, at Zion Mountain Ranch. Bison, beef, and lamb raised on Utah and Colorado ranches form the backbone of a contemporary American menu that also always features at least one vegetarian option and usually trout or salmon as well. **Known for:** great wine list; beef and bison steaks and burgers; close to Zion's East Entrance. 🔁 Average main: $29 ⊠ Zion Mountain Ranch, 9065 W. Hwy. 9, Mount Carmel Junction ☎ 435/648–2555 ⊕ www.zmr.com/dining.

🛏 Hotels

Arrowhead Country Inn & Cabins

$ | **B&B/INN** | **FAMILY** | In a lush valley framed by towering white cliffs, across the road from the Maynard Dixon and Edith Hamlin Home and Studio, this bucolic compound consists of well-appointed cabins, a verdant horse pasture, apple orchards, a pool and hot tub, and a farm market and bakery. **Pros:** delicious breakfasts and organic coffee included; kids love the farm animals and horses; some cabins have full kitchens. **Cons:** no refunds if cancelling within 21 days of arrival; few restaurants and services nearby; no pets. 🔁 Rooms from: $179 ⊠ 2155 S. State St., (U.S. 89), Mount Carmel ☎ 435/648–2569 ⊕ www.arrowheadbb.com ⇔ 11 units ◎ Free Breakfast.

Best Western East Zion Thunderbird Lodge

$ | **MOTEL** | About 13 miles beyond the East Entrance of Zion National Park, this low-slung motel with clean, spacious rooms decorated with rustic lodge-style furniture is a good option if you also want to be within an hour's drive of Bryce Canyon National Park. **Pros:** restaurant serves delicious pies; outdoor heated pool, hot tub; well-manicured grounds and nine-hole golf course. **Cons:** no elevator; limited dining options nearby; breakfast not included. 🔁 Rooms from: $159 ⊠ U.S. 89 and Hwy. 9, Mount Carmel

Junction ☎ *435/648–2203* ⊕ *www.bestwestern.com* 🛏 *61 rooms* ⵏⵣⵍ *No Meals.*

★ East Zion Resort

$$ | **RESORT** | **FAMILY** | Operated by one of the area's leading adventure tour companies, this eco-chic resort spread across three properties in the heart of Orderville offers a variety of distinctive, contemporary, and beautifully appointed accommodations, including tiny houses, treehouse-inspired lofts, and fully climate-controlled yurts and canvas glamping tents. **Pros:** excellent food-truck-style restaurant; large outdoor pool with two hot tubs; Jeep rentals available on site. **Cons:** the resort's three sections are a short drive from one another; not many dining options nearby; slightly pricey for the area. $ *Rooms from: $242* ✉ *490 E. State St., Orderville* ☎ *833/378–9466* ⊕ *www.eastzionresort.com* 🛏 *29 units* ⵏⵣⵍ *No Meals.*

Zion Mountain Ranch

$$ | **RESORT** | **FAMILY** | This peaceful ranch-style resort with more than 50 handsomely furnished cabins and lodge-style vacation homes that sleep from 2 to 15 guests lies a mere 4 miles from the East Entrance of Zion National Park and offers a variety of activities, including horseback riding, jeep tours, and guided hikes. **Pros:** rustic-chic aesthetic; spectacularly scenic surroundings; excellent restaurant. **Cons:** some decor is a bit dated; spotty Wi-Fi; half-hour drive to Kanab's restaurants. $ *Rooms from: $270* ✉ *9065 W. Hwy. 9, Mount Carmel Junction* ☎ *435/648–2555, 866/648–2555* ⊕ *www.zmr.com* 🛏 *53 cabins* ⵏⵣⵍ *No Meals.*

Zion Ponderosa Ranch Resort

$ | **RESORT** | **FAMILY** | Just a few miles beyond Zion National Park's East Entrance and about 16 miles northwest of Mount Carmel Junction, this scenic, 4,000-acre ranch offers a varied lineup of lodgings and a dizzying array of activities. **Pros:** lots of family-friendly activities; tranquil setting near Zion's East Entrance; off-season packages include breakfast and Jeep tours. **Cons:** two-night minimum; least expensive cabins lack a private bath; few dining options nearby. $ *Rooms from: $159* ✉ *Twin Knolls Rd., Mount Carmel Junction* ☎ *435/648–2700* ⊕ *www.zionponderosa. com* 🛏 *37 units* ⵏⵣⵍ *No Meals.*

 Activities

ADVENTURE TOURS

Roam Outdoor Adventure Co.

ADVENTURE TOURS | Although this outfitter that also runs Orderville's beautiful East Zion Resort offers some family-friendly, low-impact

Jeep and UTV (utility terrain vehicle) tours of slot canyons in the area, it excels with more extreme adventures—canyoneering, rappelling, and via ferrata (using iron steps to scale steep rock faces). Tours last from two to nine hours, and no experience is required for most. The company also rents electric surfboards, stand-up paddleboards, and kayaks to use on Jackson Flat Reservoir in Kanab as well as e-bikes to cruise around the reservoir. ⊠ *500 E. State St., Orderville* ☎ *855/635–9100* ⊕ *www.roam-outdoor.com* ☞ *From $49.*

HIKING
Red Hollow Canyon
HIKING & WALKING | FAMILY | For a highly rewarding and relatively easy hiking adventure close to town, take this 2-mile round-trip trek that ends in a dramatic, sheer-walled, red rock slot canyon. ⊠ *Red Hollow Dr., off 100 E.*

Kanab

21 miles south of Orderville, and 65 miles south of Panguitch.

In the 1920s, Kanab became a Hollywood vision of the American West. Soaring vermilion sandstone cliffs and sagebrush flats with endless vistas lured filmmakers to the area, which has appeared in more than 170 movies and TV shows, including *Stagecoach, My Friend Flicka, Fort Apache, The Outlaw Josey Wales, Maverick,* and many others. And although Kanab is no longer a major filming location, old movie posters and photos now cover the walls of many local businesses.

This town of about 5,000 now prospers as a convenient, scenic, and relatively affordable base for visiting three of the nation's top national parks: Zion, Bryce Canyon, and the Grand Canyon (North Rim). It's also an excellent base for visiting Grand Staircase–Escalante and Pipe Spring national monuments as well as the mesmerizing landscapes of the Paria Canyon–Vermilion Cliffs Wilderness. And it's become a mecca among animal lovers, who come here to visit Best Friends Animal Sanctuary. As the town's popularity continues to soar, Kanab has developed an impressive crop of hip boutique hotels and one of southern Utah's better restaurant scenes.

GETTING HERE AND AROUND
U.S. 89 cuts right through town, with U.S. 89A breaking off to the south into northern Arizona. You can walk to many hotels and restaurants within town, but a car is a must for exploring the area.

◉ Sights

★ Best Friends Animal Sanctuary

WILDLIFE REFUGE | **FAMILY** | On a typical day, this 3,700-acre compound 7 miles north of town houses some 1,600 rescued animals, mostly dogs and cats but also horses, rabbits, farm animals, and even wildlife in need of shelter. They receive dozens of visitors who come to take one of the free 90-minute tours (offered four times daily) or a special tour of Dogtown, Cat World Headquarters, Bunny House, Parrot Garden, or one of the other animal-specific areas of the sanctuary and to walk through the animal cemetery or even hike in adjacent Angel Canyon. Founded in 1984 and with several other adoption centers and offices around the country, Best Friends is the largest animal sanctuary in the United States and one of the world's most successful and influential no-kill animal rescue advocacy organizations. It's a rewarding visit if you love animals, and if you have the time and interest, you and your family can volunteer for a day at this amazing place. The organization also operates the Best Friends Roadhouse and Mercantile, a unique pet-centric hotel and gift shop. All tours should be booked online or by phone, even if same day. ⊠ *5001 Angel Canyon Rd., Kanab* ☎ *435/644–2001* ⊕ *bestfriends.org/sanctuary.*

Coral Pink Sand Dunes State Park

STATE/PROVINCIAL PARK | This sweeping, 3,730-acre expanse of pink sand about 20 miles west of Kanab is the result of eroding sandstone. Funneled through a notch in the rock, wind picks up speed and carries grains of sand into the area—the undulating formations can reach heights of 100 feet and move as much as 50 feet per year. It's a giant playground for dune buggies, ATVs, and dirt bikes. If you just want a quick scamper through the dunes, park in one of the small roadside lots; there's no fee collected at these areas, and they're farther away from where vehicles zoom through the sand and so tend to be quieter. Children love to play in the sand, but check the surface temperature; it can get very hot. ⊠ *Coral Sand Dunes Rd. (Hwy. 43), Kanab* ✛ *11 miles southwest of U.S. 89* ☎ *435/648–2800* ⊕ *stateparks.utah.gov/parks/coral-pink* ⌨ *$10 per vehicle.*

Kanab Heritage House Museum

HISTORIC HOME | One of the most stately residences in southern Utah, this 1890s redbrick gingerbread Victorian home in the center of town is surrounded by herb and flower gardens and contains many of the original owners' furnishings. Guided tours are offered throughout the day, and historical demonstrations are presented from time to time. Visits provide an interesting look at pioneer life in the Southwest. ⊠ *115 S. Main St., Kanab* ☎ *435/644–3506*

⊕ *www.kanabheritagehouse.com* ⊙ *Closed Sun., and Mon.–Thurs. in Oct.–mid-May.*

★ Paria Canyon–Vermilion Cliffs Wilderness

NATURE PRESERVE | In this extremely remote 112,500-acre expanse of otherworldly canyons, cliffs, and mesas that straddles the Utah–Arizona border south of Grand Staircase–Escalante National Monument, you'll find the subjects of some of the most famous and photographed rock formations in the Southwest, including The Wave, an undulating landscape of waves frozen in striated red, orange, and yellow sandstone that can be accessed by permit only—it's reached via a somewhat strenuous 6.4-mile round-trip hike. The area has a number of other spectacular features, several of them a bit easier to access, such as the moderately easy 3.7-mile Wire Pass Trail, which leads to the longest slot canyon in the world, 13-mile Buckskin Gulch.

For any visits to this wilderness, part of which falls within Vermilion Cliffs National Monument, it's essential that you check with the area's BLM ranger offices in Kanab or Big Water (near Lake Powell) for guidance and conditions (deadly flash floods can occur with little warning in some of these slot canyons); staff can also provide permit information about visiting The Wave (aka Coyote Buttes North) and Coyote Buttes South. Or consider visiting the area on tour through one of the reputable outfitters in Kanab or Escalante, such as Dreamland Safari Tours, Forever Adventure Tours, and Paria Outpost & Outfitters. The parking lot for the Wire Pass Trailhead, a good place to start your explorations of the area, is 45 miles east of Kanab via U.S. 89 (turn right onto House Rock Valley Road shortly after milemarker 26 and continue 8.5 miles down the unpaved road).

Only 64 people are granted permits to visit The Wave each day, and all are awarded by online lottery (48 of them by advanced lottery up to four months in advance, and 16 of them by daily lottery issued two days in advance). Visit ⊕ *www.blm.gov/node/7605* for details. ⊠ *Wire Pass Trailhead parking lot, House Rock Valley Rd.* ☎ *435/644–1300* ⊕ *www.blm.gov/visit/paria-canyon-vermilion-cliffs-wilderness-area* ⊠ *$6 per person day use; reservations and permits required for some hikes.*

Paria Movie Set Day Use Site

GHOST TOWN | Surrounded by stunning striated bluffs and rock formations, here in this remote valley you can visit two ghost towns at once at the Paria (sometimes called Pahreah) townsite and movie set, one settled by hardy pioneers and one built by Hollywood but lost in 1998, briefly rebuilt, and then lost to a fire in 2006. In fact, floods also caused the demise of the original

Permission to hike The Wave, a spectacular formation in Paria Canyon-Vermillion Cliffs Wilderness, is one of the toughest permits to secure in Utah.

settlements along the Paria River, with the original town fully abandoned by around 1930. Films shot here include the 1962 Rat Pack comedy *Sergeants 3*, the Gregory Peck film *Mackenna's Gold*, and the famous Clint Eastwood Civil War western, *The Outlaw Josey Wales*, which was released in 1976, making it the last of the site's movie productions. To get here, drive 33 miles east of Kanab on U.S. 89, turning left—shortly after mile marker 31—at the Old Town Paria rock marker, and following the unpaved road about 4½ miles north to the parking area and wooden restroom. ⊠ *Paria Valley Rd.* ☎ *435/644–1300* ⊕ *www.blm.gov/ visit/paria-movie-set-day-use-site.*

Pipe Spring National Monument

NATIONAL PARK | A 20-minute drive southwest of Kanab, this 40-acre plot of stone buildings and sagebrush- and red rock–dotted hillsides with a pond and gardens preserves a site where indigenous Kaibab Paiute people thrived for a thousand years, followed by Spanish missionaries and Mormon pioneers in the mid-19th century. A modern visitor center contains artifacts and interactive exhibits and presents a short video detailing the history of this community and its reliance on the natural springs that run beneath it. Rangers give guided tours and crafts demonstrations during the summer months, but any time of year you can explore the grounds, buildings, orchards, and horse and cattle corrals on your own and hike the ½-mile Ridge Trail for an astounding view of the Arizona Strip, as this region is known. ⊠ *406 N. Pipe Springs Rd., off Hwy. 389* ☎ *928/643–7105* ⊕ *www.nps.gov/pisp* ⊠ *$10.*

🍴 Restaurants

Peekaboo Canyon Wood Fired Kitchen
$ | **VEGETARIAN** | This inviting, art-filled restaurant at the Flagstone Inn has one of the only all-vegetarian menus in southern Utah, but even avowed carnivores have been known to rave about the green chile–and–Swiss cheese Impossible burgers and the inventive pizzas—including the "hot mess," with vegan Italian sausage, chèvre, shishito and serrano peppers, and a bourbon sauce. There's an impressive selection of craft beers and ciders. **Known for:** large patio with sandstone tables; Impossible burgers and meatballs; salted-caramel crunch cake for dessert. ⑤ *Average main: $17* ✉ *The Flagstone Boutique Inn & Suites, 233 W. Center St., Kanab* ☎ *435/689–1959* ⊕ *www.peekabookitchen.com* ☾ *Closed Sun. and Mon. No lunch.*

Rocking V Cafe
$$ | **SOUTHWESTERN** | This upbeat, art-filled eatery inside the town's former post office focuses on slow-cooked meals made from scratch, such as the Kanab-A-Dabba-A-Doo burger, a half-pound patty topped with Hatch chilies, bacon, cheddar, and avocado, and a chargrilled bison tenderloin with a fig demi-glace. Several excellent vegan options are available, too, such as yellow coconut curry with miso-marinated tofu. **Known for:** excellent margaritas; attractive patio; bread pudding with rotating preparations. ⑤ *Average main: $25* ✉ *97 W. Center St., Kanab* ☎ *435/644–8001* ⊕ *www.rockingvcafe.com* ☾ *Closed Tues. and Wed.*

★ Sego
$$ | **MODERN AMERICAN** | Folks have been known to drive for an hour or more to partake of the outstanding modern American and Asian fare served in this charmingly intimate dining room just off the lobby of the romantic Canyons Boutique Hotel in Kanab. The small-plates–focused menu here changes often according to what's fresh, but recent standouts have included wok-fry rice noodles with Hawaiian red crab and curry oil, and seared duck-breast lo mein with sambal and jalapeño cream. **Known for:** creative, globally inspired cooking; stellar wine and cocktail list; romantic yet unfussy vibe. ⑤ *Average main: $22* ✉ *Canyons Boutique Hotel, 190 N. 300 W, Kanab* ☎ *435/644–5680* ⊕ *www.segokanab.com* ☾ *Closed Sun. and Thurs. No lunch.*

★ Vermillion 45
$$ | **MEDITERRANEAN** | The sophisticated contemporary Mediterranean fare served in this snazzy bistro with a cathedral ceiling and an open kitchen would hold its own in any big city. Start off your evening with escargot with herbed garlic butter or French onion

soup, before graduating to gnocchi with sautéed lobster tail or pan-seared duck breast with a cherry reduction and truffle-dusted potatoes. **Known for:** charcuterie and cheese boards; outstanding wine and cocktail selection; house-made gelato. $ *Average main: $23* ⊠ *210 S. 100 E* ☎ *435/644–3300* ⊕ *www.vermillion45.com* ⊗ *Closed Mon. and Tues.*

Wild Thyme Cafe

$$ | **MODERN AMERICAN** | Using herbs and produce from the on-site organic garden and sourcing meat and seafood from top-quality purveyors, the kitchen at this contemporary neighborhood bistro serves up delicious Southwestern fare. Fire-grilled Idaho trout and slow-braised, chargrilled cowboy pork ribs with barbecue sauce and an agave-mustard vinaigrette are a couple of house specialties, and there's also a nice selection of bowls featuring sesame tofu, falafel cakes, Jamaican-spiced pork, and other tasty proteins. **Known for:** pretty deck with red rock views; outstanding list of creative cocktails; salted-caramel cheesecake. $ *Average main: $27* ⊠ *198 S. 100 E, Kanab* ☎ *435/644–2848* ⊕ *www. wildthymekanab.com.*

☕ Coffee and Quick Bites

★ Kanab Creek Bakery

$ | **CAFÉ** | Drop by this intimate and urbane bakery-café with an expansive patio for some of the tastiest breakfast and lunch fare for miles around, as well as fine espresso drinks, teas, raw juice blends, and a small but well-chosen selection of beer and wine. **Known for:** cheerful patio (but limited indoor) seating; heavenly croissants, Belgian chocolate chip cookies, and other sweet treats; fantastic breakfasts. $ *Average main: $10* ⊠ *238 W. Center St., Kanab* ☎ *435/644–5689* ⊕ *www.kanabcreekbakery.com* ⊗ *Closed Mon. and Tues. No dinner.*

🛏 Hotels

★ Best Friends Roadhouse and Mercantile

$ | **MOTEL** | The nationally renowned, Kanab-based Best Friends Animal Society runs this smartly designed, pet-centric motel that offers a slew of amenities for travelers with four-legged friends, including a fenced dog park and water feature, pet treats and beds, built-in cubbies for snuggling and napping, and dog-walking and pet-visit services. **Pros:** hip, modern design; pets stay free (up to four, of any size); staying here supports a great cause. **Cons:** not a great fit if you're not a fan of pets; on a busy road; lacks a full-service restaurant. $ *Rooms from: $153* ⊠ *30 N. 300 W*

☎ 435/644–3400 ⊕ www.bestfriendsroadhouse.org ⤳ 40 rooms ⦿| Free Breakfast.

★ The Canyons Lodge

$ | HOTEL | With cattle-print throw pillows, papier-mâché mounted deer heads, log walls, and custom beds with rattan or carved-wood headboards, the playful vibe at this quirky 16-room boutique inn sets it apart from the usual budget-friendly lodgings in the Zion and Bryce area. **Pros:** fun and quirky ambience; good base for Zion, Bryce, and the North Rim of the Grand Canyon; there's a small pool. **Cons:** the least expensive rooms are tiny; complimentary breakfast is at nearby sister property; some road noise. ⑤ Rooms from: $114 ⊠ 236 N. 300 W ☎ 435/644–3069 ⊕ www. canyonslodge.com ⤳ 16 rooms ⦿| Free Breakfast.

Parry Lodge

$ | HOTEL | Constructed in 1929, this landmark lodge hosted dozens of movie stars during Kanab's movie location heyday and is now a fun and simple, well-located base for budget-minded parks visitors. **Pros:** fascinating "old Hollywood" ambience; large pool; reasonably priced. **Cons:** some rooms are quite small; no elevator; breakfast costs extra. ⑤ Rooms from: $104 ⊠ 89 E. Center St., Kanab ☎ 435/644–2601 ⊕ parrylodge.com ⤳ 89 rooms ⦿| No Meals.

Activities

HIKING

Sand Caves

HIKING & WALKING | FAMILY | A little north of town and not to be confused with the touristy Moqui Cave, which is less than a mile up the road, these man-made sandstone caves were created in the early 1970s as part of a sand-mining operation and are reached via a slightly steep half-mile scramble. It's fun exploring these caverns and gazing out at the pinyon-dotted hills below. ⊠ U.S. 89 at Angel Canyon Rd.

★ Squaw Trail

HIKING & WALKING | FAMILY | With a trailhead right on the north side of downtown, this rugged 3-mile round-trip hike offers tremendous views of the Kanab valley and the surrounding high-desert landscape. Although a bit steep in places, the total elevation gain of about 800 feet is manageable for most, and the trail is very well-maintained—and the eye-popping scenery is worth the effort, especially considering how much less crowded this trail is than those at nearby national parks. ⊠ N. 100 E at W. 600 N.

ADVENTURE TOURS
★ Dreamland Safari Tours

ADVENTURE TOURS | This long-respected Kanab-based outfitter with around 20 super-knowledgeable guides offers myriad half- and full-day excursions throughout the surrounding countryside, from slot canyon and sunset photography trips near town to adventures a bit farther afield. Tours take place in the Paria Canyon Wilderness and Vermilion Cliffs National Monument, in Grand Staircase–Escalante National Monument, and around the North Rim of the Grand Canyon and nearby Marble Canyon. Multiday "desert safari" and photography tours are offered as well. ☎ *435/291–1083* ⊕ *dreamlandtours.net* ✉ *From $99.*

★ Paria Outpost & Outfitters

ADVENTURE TOURS | Husband-and-wife owners Steve and Susan Dodson and their small team of guides are among the best experts on the Paria Canyon–Vermilion Cliffs Wilderness area and Grand Staircase–Escalante National Monument (especially the southern sections). The company offers photo workshops and guided tours of all the key destinations in these wilderness areas, including The Wave, as well as shuttle services if you're doing a one-way hike through Buckskin Gulch or Paria Canyon. Note that all services are cash only. ✉ *U.S. 89, between mile makers 21 and 22* ☎ *928/691–1047* ⊕ *www.paria.com* ✉ *From $125.*

BRYCE CANYON NATIONAL PARK

Updated by
Andrew Collins

⛰ **Camping**
★★★★★

🛏 **Hotels**
★★★★☆

🏃 **Activities**
★★★★★

👁 **Scenery**
★★★★★

👥 **Crowds**
★★☆☆☆

WELCOME TO BRYCE CANYON NATIONAL PARK

TOP REASONS TO GO

★ **Hoodoo heaven:** The boldly colored, gravity-defying limestone tentacles reaching skyward—called hoodoos—are Bryce Canyon's most recognizable attraction.

★ **Famously fresh air:** With some of the clearest skies in the nation, the park offers views that, on a clear day, can extend nearly 200 miles and into three states.

★ **Spectacular sunrises and sunsets:** The deep orange and crimson hues of the park's hoodoos are intensified by the light of the sun at either end of the day.

★ **Dramatically different zones:** From the highest point of the rim to the canyon base, the park spans 2,000 feet, so you can explore three unique climatic zones: spruce-fir forest, ponderosa-pine forest, and pinyon–juniper forest.

★ **Snowy fun:** Bryce gets nearly 100 inches of snowfall a year and is a popular destination for skiers and snowshoe enthusiasts.

1 Bryce Canyon North. From this, the heart of the park, you can access the most famous sites in Bryce Amphitheater, including the historic Lodge at Bryce Canyon as well as Sunrise, Sunset, and Inspiration Points. Walk to Bryce Point at sunrise to view the mesmerizing collection of massive hoodoos known as Silent City.

2 Under-the-Rim. The best way to reach the backcountry is along this 23-mile trail. It offers the chance for anything from a challenging three-day adventure to a few hours of fun from one of four main-road access points. Primitive campgrounds dot the route.

3 Rainbow and Yovimpa Points. At the end of the scenic road, you can hike an easy trail to see ancient bristlecone pines and look southeast into Grand Staircase–Escalante National Monument.

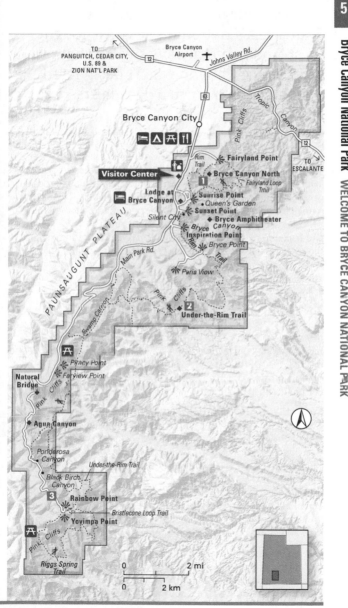

A land that captures the imagination and the heart, Bryce is a favorite among the Southwest's national parks. Although its splendor has always rivaled that of Zion, Bryce Canyon wasn't designated a national park until a decade after its sibling.

The park is named for hard-luck pioneer rancher Ebenezer Bryce, who famously remarked that the Bryce Amphitheater, the semicircular bowl-shape area that contains the park's most famous geologic wonders, is "a hell of a place to lose a cow." A Scottish immigrant sent to the area by the Mormon Church to begin an agricultural community, he created an irrigation ditch for his crops and built a road through the cliffs to make it easier to transport timber from the forests. The road ended at the amphitheater, and people started calling the area "Bryce's Canyon." Finding the locale inhospitable to successful farming, Bryce departed the valley below the canyon (for Arizona) five years after arriving, as did other settlers.

In the early 1900s, conservationists concerned about damage to the lands—from overuse by visitors and increased logging—lobbied for federal protection of the area. The government responded in 1923, first by designating it a national monument, and then, a year later, by establishing it as Utah National Park. It was given its current name in 1928.

Within Bryce's approximately 56 square miles (about one-fourth the size of Zion) lie three distinct temperate zones; countless species of birds, animals, and flora; a scenic drive; more than a dozen trails; and tens of millions of years of geological history. Among the byproducts of this history are Bryce Canyon's fanciful rock formations known as hoodoos, which are particularly spectacular at sunrise and sunset when the light plays off the red rock. Bryce continues to evolve today, with old hoodoos crumbling (as erosion undercuts the soft rock beneath the harder, caprock top layer) and new ones forming as the amphitheater rim recedes.

The high plateau—traversed by a scenic drive and home to the visitor center and the Lodge at Bryce Canyon—is named Paunsaugunt, the Paiute word for "home of the beaver." At an elevation of more than 8,000 feet, it's covered by hardy pines, inhabited

AVERAGE HIGH/LOW TEMPERATURES (FAHRENHEIT)					
Jan.	Feb.	Mar.	Apr.	May	June
37/15	38/17	45/23	54/29	64/37	75/45
July	Aug.	Sept.	Oct.	Nov.	Dec.
80/53	77/50	70/42	58/32	45/23	36/15

by deer and small mammals, and surrounded by clean air. Its rim gives way to an otherworldly landscape that attracts nearly 2.5 million visitors per year.

Planning

When to Go

Within Bryce Canyon National Park, elevations surpass 9,000 feet, making for temperamental weather, intermittent and seasonal road closures due to snow, and downright cold nights well into June. The air is cooler on the plateau above the canyon than it is at lower altitudes.

■ TIP→ **April through October, and especially summer, is high season in the park. Traffic can be heavy and parking limited during this period, so consider getting around on the free park shuttle bus. Also at this time, RV access is limited to a handful of lots and camping areas, most of them near the park entrance.**

Free from crowds, Bryce is an underrated delight between November and February (although the park lodge and restaurants are closed during this time). You have trails to yourself in winter, and the park's dramatic features are stunning under a fresh layer of snow. Keep in mind that the main park road does sometimes close, especially south of Rainbow Gate, when there's heavy snow.

Getting Here and Around

AIR

The nearest commercial airports to Bryce Canyon are tiny Cedar City Regional Airport (an hour and 45 minutes), which has twice-daily flights on Delta to Salt Lake City, and St. George Regional Airport (2½ hours), which has daily service to Salt Lake City, Phoenix, and Denver. The nearest major airports to Bryce are Salt Lake City (4 to 4½ hours) and Las Vegas (about 4½ to 5

Great Itineraries

Bryce Canyon in One Day

Begin your day at the **visitor center** just past the park entrance. Pick up the latest park guide and Junior Ranger booklets for the kids, and watch the 24-minute overview film. Sign up for a ranger-led hike or talk—these are always tremendously fun and informative for adults as well as families.

Try to beat the crowds by driving early to the park's south end for your first full look into the canyon at **Rainbow Point**. From here, a short, rolling hike along the **Bristlecone Loop** trail takes you through a forest of these gnarled namesake pines and rewards you with spectacular views. You can see east into Grand Staircase–Escalante National Monument and west across the Paunsaugunt Plateau, and on clear days, the view extends south as far as the Grand Canyon.

Start working your way back to **Bryce Point**, allowing two to three hours for the drive and stops at some of the key viewpoints, such as **Agua Canyon**, **Natural Bridge**, and **Paria View**. This timing will enable you to spend the latter half of the day at the **Bryce Amphitheater** at the heart of the park. Begin your explorations with lunch at the **Lodge at Bryce Canyon**, or pick up snacks at the park's **General Store**.

Enjoy a relaxing hike along the **Rim Trail**, then drop down into the canyon on one of the park's signature short hikes. The easiest route is the **Queen's Garden Trail** at Sunrise Point. If you're a little more ambitious, take the steep switchbacks of the **Navajo Loop** to **Wall Street**. Remember that almost all Bryce hikes feature a sharp descent into the canyon at the outset, which unfortunately means a rigorous climb to exit. This part of the plateau lies around 8,000 feet, so be prepared for the thin air and risk of sunburn.

End your day with dinner at the **Lodge at Bryce Canyon**. Try to time sunset to be at an overlook: **Inspiration Point**, **Sunset Point**, and **Bryce Point** all offer memorable vistas. If you can't have dinner at the lodge (which is first-come, first-served), **Bryce Canyon Pines Restaurant** and **i.d.k. Barbecue** are good, reasonably priced options within a 20-minute drive of the park.

Bryce Canyon in Three Days

Staying inside the park at the **Lodge at Bryce Canyon** (reserve at least four months in advance if possible) or in a nearby town will help you maximize your time exploring Bryce's attractions over three days.

On your first morning, try to get to the **visitor center** when it opens (at 8 am) to get oriented and choose one of the ranger-led talks or hikes available that day. Then head to **Bryce Amphitheater** to begin a combination hike from **Sunrise Point** along the connected **Queen's Garden** and **Navajo Loop** trails. You can see Queen Victoria, Thor's Hammer, and Wall Street, three of the park's icons. Relax and recover from this moderate hike with a picnic lunch or a meal at the **Lodge and Bryce Canyon** and then take the 18-mile scenic drive, stopping to see **Agua Canyon, Natural Bridge,** and **Bryce Point.** Wherever you are on the plateau, keep your eyes open for deer, prairie dogs, and dozens of bird species. Have dinner, on the patio if it's not too cool outside, at **Valhalla Pizzeria,** next to the Lodge at Bryce Canyon. Get to sleep early, in anticipation of rising very early the following day.

On Day 2, get to **Sunrise Point** at least a half-hour before dawn breaks so that you can watch the event for which this dramatic promontory on the amphitheater rim is named. Then descend into the canyon for a half-day hike. The **Peekaboo Loop** (three to four hours) takes you to see The Wall of Windows; the **Fairyland Loop** (four to five hours) takes you to the Tower Bridge and the China Wall; the **Agua Canyon Connecting Trail** (four to five hours; but check before you go, as this trail was closed for

renovations as of this writing) gives you a taste of the famed Under-the-Rim Trail and a view of Natural Bridge from below. End your day with dinner at the **Lodge at Bryce Canyon**—be prepared for a possible wait, as seating is first-come, first-served. If the wait is too long, head to one of the key overlooks to watch the sunset—**Inspiration Point, Sunset Point,** or **Bryce Point**—and either try again for a table at the lodge or have dinner in one of the restaurants outside the park.

On your final day, savor the perspectives from **Fairyland Point** or **Bryce Point,** then return to scenic **Highway 12.** If you're headed west—toward Zion or Cedar Breaks, for example—spend an hour or two exploring **Red Canyon** (10 miles west of the junction with Highway 63) in Dixie National Forest; the 1.7-mile round-trip Bird's Eye Trail is a kid-friendly hike from the informative visitor center. Save room for a slice of homemade pie at **Bryce Canyon Pines Restaurant.** If you're headed east—toward Grand Staircase–Escalante or Capitol Reef—hike the underrated **Mossy Cave Trail** (within Bryce Canyon National Park but accessible only from Highway 12), a short, 0.8-mile round-trip that showcases Bryce's floral diversity and a small waterfall. Have dinner in Tropic at the upscale **Stone Hearth Grille** or the casual **i.d.k. Barbecue.**

hours). The most direct route to St. George and Las Vegas passes through Zion, making those airports a good choice if you're visiting that park as well.

BUS

A free shuttle bus operates in Bryce Canyon from early April through late October. Buses start at 8 am and run every 10 to 15 minutes until 8 pm in summer and 6 pm in spring and fall; you must show a receipt confirming that you've paid the park admission in order to board. The route begins at the Shuttle Station north of the park in Bryce Canyon City, where parking is available, and also stops at the hotels and campground in town. Upon entering the park, the shuttle stops at all the key points of interest, including the visitor center, lodge, campgrounds, and main overlooks and trailheads in Bryce Amphitheater (the shuttle goes only as far as Bryce Point and Paria View).

National Park Express offers bus shuttle service between Bryce Canyon City (just outside the park) and St. George, stopping in Zion National Park as well. From there, St. George Shuttle offers regularly scheduled bus service to the airports in Las Vegas and Salt Lake City.

CAR

Most visitors to Bryce arrive by car, since they're typically also exploring southern Utah's other national parks and attractions. But if you're visiting only Bryce (and the central areas of Zion), it's definitely possible to do so using the shuttles described above. Even if you arrive by car, during the busy spring–fall high season, it makes sense to leave your vehicle in Bryce Canyon City and use the free park shuttle to get around; in addition to cutting down on congestion, you'll avoid heavy traffic and the hassle of limited parking spaces.

To drive to the park, it's about a four- to five-hour drive from either Salt Lake City or Las Vegas. Bryce's only entrance is via Highway 63, just off of Highway 12, which leads west to U.S. 89 just south of Panguitch (a 20-minute drive), from which you can continue toward Cedar Breaks, Zion, or even the North Rim of the Grand Canyon (via Kanab). Or you can head east on Highway 12 for the spectacular drive through Grand Staircase–Escalante National Monument and Capitol Reef National Park, which is just outside Torrey, a little under a three-hour drive. Bryce's well-maintained main road, also referred to as the scenic drive, makes for a gorgeous drive year-round, but again, during busier periods, increased traffic can make taking the free shuttle bus a better option.

Inspiration

Shadows of Time: The Geology of Bryce Canyon National Park, by Frank Decourten with photographs by John Telford, explains regional geology and points out things to look for at park overlooks.

Supplement the free park map with Trails Illustrated's *Bryce Canyon Map,* which is produced by National Geographic and includes a detailed park hiking map, trail descriptions, and photographs.

A fun and enlightening resource geared to kids up to around age 10 is *Bryce Canyon,* by Jennifer Hackett, part of a series called "A True Book: National Parks" that depicts park history, geology, scenery, plants, and animals. The series also includes books on both Zion and the Grand Canyon.

You can find all of these titles at major booksellers or purchase them from the nonprofit Bryce Canyon Association (⊕ *www. brycecanyon.org*), either online or in person at the bookstore they operate at the park's visitor center.

Park Essentials

ACCESSIBILITY
Although most park facilities were constructed between 1920 and 1960, many have been upgraded for wheelchair accessibility (some requiring assistance). Sunset Campground has two sites designed and reserved for visitors with mobility impairments, and these are across from an accessible restroom. Most restrooms in the park have accessible stalls, and the visitor center can be accessed by wheelchair. Few of Bryce's typically steep or rocky trails, however, are conducive for wheelchairs, with the exception of the paved half-mile span of the Rim Trail between Sunrise and Inspiration Points. Additionally, the 1-mile Bristlecone Loop at Rainbow Point has a hard surface and is wheelchair-accessible with assistance, as several grades do not meet accessibility standards. All of the park's main viewpoints and public facilities have ramps and accessible parking spaces.

CELL PHONE RECEPTION
Cell phone reception is generally reliable just outside the park in Bryce Canyon City but is hit-or-miss inside the park, with some of the higher points along the main road your best bet. The lodge and visitor center have limited (it can be slow during busy periods) Wi-Fi.

PARK FEES

The entrance fee for Bryce Canyon National Park is $35 per vehicle (or party using the park's free shuttle bus), $30 per motorcycle, and $20 per person entering on foot or by bicycle and is good for seven days.

A backcountry permit, available from the visitor center or online in advance from ⊕ *www.recreation.gov,* is required for camping in the park's interior, allowed only on the Under-the-Rim Trail and the Riggs Spring Loop. The cost is $10 to apply for the permit, and then $5 for each person in your party to obtain it.

PARK HOURS

The park, open daily year-round, 24 hours a day, is in the Mountain Time Zone.

Hotels

Lodgings in and around Bryce Canyon include both rustic and modern options, but all fill up fast in summer and even on spring and fall weekends. The Lodge at Bryce Canyon, which is closed from November through March, is the only hotel inside the park. There are a few accommodations of varying quality in Bryce Canyon City, just north of the park's entrance. Nearby Tropic and Panguitch each have a handful of decent options, and a bit farther, Escalante to the east and Orderville and Kanab to the southwest (and en route to Zion and the Grand Canyon's North Rim) offer more varied choices, from simple motels to upscale glamping compounds and boutique inns. Other gateway towns include Cedar City and smaller Brian Head, which are about 90 minutes away but very close to Cedar Breaks National Monument and Interstate 15.

Restaurants

Dining options in the park proper are limited to a few options at the Lodge at Bryce Canyon; you'll also find a handful of pretty mediocre options just outside the park in Bryce Canyon City. These are okay in a pinch, but you'll find tastier fare as you venture farther afield—to Tropic and Escalante to the east, and Panguitch and Kanab to the west and southwest.

⇨ *Hotel and restaurant reviews have been shortened. For full information, visit Fodors.com. Restaurant prices are the average cost of a main course at dinner, or if dinner is not served, at lunch.*

Hotel prices are the average cost of a standard double room in high season, excluding taxes and service charges.

What It Costs			
$	$$	$$$	$$$$
RESTAURANTS			
under $20	$20–$30	$31–$40	over $40
HOTELS			
under $200	$200–$350	$351–$500	over $500

Tours

★ Full Moon Hike

WALKING TOURS | Rangers lead guided one- to two-hour hikes on the nights around each full moon (two per month). You must wear heavy-traction shoes and reserve a spot on the day of the hike at the visitor center, which distributes tickets by lottery at 4 pm. The hikes depart around sunset. No flashlights or head lamps are allowed, and children must be at least 8 years old. ⊠ *Bryce Canyon National Park* ⊕ *www.nps.gov/brca/planyourvisit/rang-er-programs.htm.*

Rim Walk with a Ranger

WALKING TOURS | **FAMILY** | Join a park ranger for a ½-mile, 45- to 60-minute-long stroll along the breathtaking rim of Bryce Canyon starting at the Sunset Point overlook. These tours are offered at 2 pm each afternoon from late May through early September, and reservations aren't needed. In winter, when snow levels allow, this becomes a snowshoe hike (for ages 8 and up only) with a longer duration (about 1½ to 2 hours). ⊠ *Bryce Canyon National Park* ⊕ *www.nps.gov/brca/planyourvisit/ranger-programs.htm.*

Ruby's Guided ATV Tours

ADVENTURE TOURS | Adventure seekers can take to the trails above the rim on ATVs from April through October, weather permitting. A local guide leads the way. Drivers must have a driver's license and be at least 16 years old and accompanied by an adult if under 18. Passengers must be at least 7 years old. ATVs carry from two to six people, including the driver. Wear long pants or jeans and closed-toe shoes; all other gear is provided. ⊠ *Bryce Canyon Auto Care Center, 105 S. Main St., Bryce Canyon City* ☎ *435/834–5231* ⊕ *www.rubysinn.com/activities-in-bryce-canyon/guided-atv-tours* ▥ *From $90.*

Bryce Canyon North

Visitor Information

CONTACTS Bryce Canyon National Park. ✉ *Hwy. 63, Bryce Canyon National Park* ☎ *435/834–5322* ⊕ *www.nps.gov/brca.*

Bryce Canyon North

This is the most popular part of the park, and its social and scenic focal point, Bryce Amphitheater, can get crowded. Here you'll find the visitor center, the lodge, both campgrounds, and the park's most celebrated trails and viewpoints. A convenient free shuttle runs a loop through this area, stopping at eight main spots where you can get out and explore. It also connects with the nearby town of Bryce Canyon City, so you don't need to bring your vehicle.

The 23-mile Under-the-Rim Trail, Bryce Canyon's longest, leads under the rim of the park's plateau and edges this natural amphitheater. Hiking the entire trail requires an overnight stay, but you can connect with it via some shorter trails in the park. On clear nights, the stargazing can be amazing.

👁 Sights

Bryce Canyon consists of a scenic drive and a fanciful world of below-the-rim formations, all layered in the context of a peaceful park setting and one of the country's foremost windows into our planet's geologic history.

Visitors enter from the north via Highway 63, just off Highway 12, a national scenic byway that crisscrosses the Grand Staircase–Escalante National Monument. With little buildup, the community of Bryce Canyon City (aka Ruby's Inn) greets you just outside the park boundary with a menagerie of hotels, tourist services, and garish signage. Travel another 2 miles to reach the entrance booth, visitor center, and primary park services.

What's a 👁 Hoodoo?

[hoo'doo] 1. n. A pinnacle or odd-shape rock left standing by the forces of erosion. 2. v. To cast a spell or cause bad luck. 3. Voodoo.

Ask park rangers and you will get different answers. Sometimes we think they like to tease visitors with playful stories, but the fact is, the name is attributed to various times and sources. Certainly it rolls off the tongue and is more fun for kids to say than, "Hey Mom—check out that eroded rock formation!"

On the park's 36-mile round-trip scenic drive, plan to make up to 13 stops to see the marvelous amphitheaters of Bryce from various perspectives. The area around the Lodge at Bryce Canyon has a general store and the most prominent trailheads.

Although the park is open 365 days a year, many services inside the park usually close around early November due to the nearly 100 inches of snow this plateau receives. As a result, most visitors visit from April through October. Come any other time of the year for fewer human encounters and plentiful tranquility.

Remember that the plateau averages more than 8,000 feet above sea level, so persons with heart or breathing conditions should use care on hikes and other forms of physical exertions. Even physically fit, active adults can experience headaches, dizziness, and other symptoms of altitude sickness here.

HISTORICAL SIGHTS

★ The Lodge at Bryce Canyon

NOTABLE BUILDING | Architect Gilbert Stanley Underwood was already a national park specialist, having designed lodges at Zion and the Grand Canyon, before turning his T square to Bryce in

1924. With its distinctive, wavy, hunter-green shingle roof and artful interior, this National Historic Landmark has been faithfully restored, right down to the lobby's huge limestone fireplace and log and wrought-iron chandelier. Inside the historic building, the only remaining hotel built by the Grand Circle Utah Parks Company, are a restaurant and gift shop, comfy sitting areas, and information on park activities. Just a short walk from the rim trail, the lodge's landscaped brick terrace is an enchanting place to relax after a hike. The lodge also offers accommodations in several historic log cabins and two lodge-inspired but motel-style buildings nearby on the wooded grounds. ⊠ *Bryce Canyon National Park* ⚓ *Off Main Park Rd.* ☎ *435/834–8700* ⊕ *www.visitbrycecanyon. com* ☙ *Closed Nov.–Mar.*

PICNIC AREAS
North Campground Picnic Area
NATURE SIGHT | This area amid many ponderosa pines has picnic tables and grills usable by non-campers. ⊠ *Main Park Rd., Bryce Canyon National Park* ⚓ *Approx. ¼ mile south of Bryce Canyon National Park Visitor Center.*

SCENIC DRIVES
★ Main Park Road
SCENIC DRIVE | Snaking for 18 miles along the canyon's rim, the park's only true thoroughfare accesses more than a dozen scenic overlooks between the entrance and Rainbow Point. Major overlooks are rarely more than a few minutes walk from the parking areas, and from many of these spots, you can see more than 100 miles on clear days. Remember that all overlooks lie east of the road, meaning that you may be looking into the sun early in the day but can enjoy spectacular color and light closer to dusk. Allow two to three hours to travel the entire 36-mile round-trip—more if you set out on any hikes along the way. The road is open year-round but sometimes closes temporarily after heavy snowfalls. Be on the lookout for wildlife crossing the road. Trailers are not allowed at Bryce Point and Paria View, and vehicles longer than 20 feet are prohibited from parking at most of the major stops in and around the Bryce Amphitheater from mid-May through late October; during these months, you can travel throughout the park via the free shuttle and park your larger vehicle at the shuttle station parking lot in Bryce Canyon City. ⊠ *(Hwy. 63), Bryce Canyon National Park.*

SCENIC STOPS
Bryce Point
VIEWPOINT | Reached via a narrow 2-mile spur road off the main park road, Bryce Point is where the park's fairly easy Rim Trail

The arch tunnel at Red Canyon serves as an "entrance" to the 124-mile Scenic Highway 12.

(which you can hike from here to Inspiration Point or even all the way to Sunrise Point) meets with the more challenging and remote Under-the-Rim Trail, and it's also the southernmost vista point into the Bryce Amphitheater—and a favorite place to watch the sunrise. After absorbing views of the Black Mountains and Navajo Mountain, you can follow the Under-the-Rim Trail to explore beyond the Bryce Amphitheater to the cluster of top-heavy hoodoos known collectively as The Hat Shop. Or, take a left off the Under-the-Rim Trail and hike the challenging Peekaboo Loop down into the amphitheater. ⊠ *Bryce Point Rd., 5 miles south of park entrance, Bryce Canyon National Park*

Fairyland Point

VIEWPOINT | The viewpoint nearest to the park entrance, this scenic overlook adjacent to Boat Mesa, ½ mile north of the visitor center and a mile off the main park road, has splendid views of Fairyland Canyon and its delicate, fanciful forms. The Sinking Ship and other formations stand before the grand backdrop of the Aquarius Plateau and distant Navajo Mountain. Nearby is the Fairyland Loop trailhead—it's a stunning five-hour hike, and in winter it's a favorite trail for snowshoeing. ⊠ *Bryce Canyon National Park* ⊕ *Off Main Park Rd.*

★ Inspiration Point

VIEWPOINT | One of the best—though often most crowded—places in the park to watch the sunset, this lofty promontory with sweeping vistas into the Bryce Amphitheater is easily accessed by car—the parking lot is down a short and well-signed spur

Bryce Canyon Geology 👁

It's hard to imagine a prehistoric freshwater lake covering much of Utah and the Southwest, but geologists are certain of its former presence. More than 65 million years ago, a network of rivers carried a variety of sediments including iron (yellow and red) and manganese (pink and violet), combining with calcium carbonate (cream) to create Bryce's signature colored limestone. This 1,300-foot deep layer is known as the Claron Formation.

Less than 15 million years ago, an uplift in the Colorado Plateau created a series of smaller plateaus, including the Paunsaugunt (the "rim" of Bryce Canyon) and Table Cliffs (the stunning formation visible as you look east). Water then shaped Bryce's accelerated erosion, not by its volume (a mere 18 inches of precipitation annually), but by the freezing and thawing that takes place more than 200 nights per year.

Finally, streams of water trickle down Bryce's rim forming gullies, cutting deep, narrow channels (called fins) into walls of rock. The fins develop windows, which grow larger (like Natural Bridge) until the roof collapses, creating a hoodoo.

road near the start of Bryce Point Road. But for a more exciting approach and a bit of fresh air and exercise, consider hiking to this dramatic spot via the relatively easy and flat Rim Trail; from Sunset Point, it's a ¾-mile trek south, and from Bryce Point, it's a 1½-mile hike northwest. From either direction, the views are spectacular for virtually the entire hike. ⊠ *Inspiration Point Rd., Bryce Canyon National Park.*

North Campground Viewpoint
VIEWPOINT | **FAMILY** | Across the road and slightly east of the Bryce Canyon Visitor Center, this popular campground has a couple of scenic picnic areas plus a general store and easy access to the Rim Trail and Sunrise Point. ⊠ *N. Campground Rd., Bryce Canyon National Park.*

★ Sunrise Point
VIEWPOINT | Named for its stunning views at dawn, this overlook a short walk from the Lodge at Bryce Canyon is one of the park's most beloved stops. It's also the trailhead for the Queen's Garden Trail and the southern end of the Fairyland Loop. You can also walk to Sunrise Point along the easy Rim Trail from Sunset Point (to the south) or North Campground (to the north). ⊠ *Sunrise Point Rd., Bryce Canyon National Park.*

Sunset Point

VIEWPOINT | Watch the late-day sun paint the hoodoos from this famous overlook a short walk from the Lodge at Bryce Canyon (or you can drive here via the short spur road off the main park road). You'll be treated to a striking view of Thor's Hammer, a delicate formation similar to a balanced rock. Sunset Point is also the access point for the tremendously popular hike 550 feet down into the amphitheater on the Navajo Loop. ⊠ *Sunset Point Rd., Bryce Canyon National Park.*

TRAILS

Fairyland Loop

TRAIL | Hike into whimsical Fairyland Canyon on this trail that gets more strenuous and less crowded as you progress along its 8 miles. It winds around hoodoos and across trickles of water, finally arriving at a natural window in the rock at the Tower Bridge, 1½ miles from Sunrise Point and 4 miles from Fairyland Point. The pink-and-white badlands and hoodoos surround you the whole way. Don't feel like you have to go the whole distance to make it worthwhile. But if you do, allow at least five hours round-trip, with 1,900 feet of elevation change. *Difficult.* ⊠ *Bryce Canyon National Park* ✛ *Trailheads: At Fairyland Point and Sunrise Point.*

Mossy Cave Trail

TRAIL | **FAMILY** | This short hike (0.8 mile) has a little bit of everything you might be looking for in Bryce: the sound of rushing water, a small waterfall, a grotto, and hoodoos. The trailhead is on Highway 12, north and east of the main entrance, and it follows an irrigation ditch dug in the 1920s by farmers from the nearby town of Tropic looking to divert water from the Sevier River for agriculture. Since the dig predates the park, the water right of way belongs to the farmers. This is an especially fun hike in winter, when the waterfall transforms into a display of dazzling icicles. *Easy.* ⊠ *Hwy. 12, Bryce Canyon National Park* ✛ *Trailhead: 3.7 miles southeast of the junction of with Hwy. 63.*

Navajo Loop

TRAIL | **FAMILY** | One of Bryce's most popular and dramatic attractions is this steep descent via a series of switchbacks leading to Wall Street, a slightly claustrophobic hallway of rock only 20 feet wide in places, with walls 100 feet high. After a walk through The Silent City, the northern end of the trail brings Thor's Hammer into view. A well-marked intersection offers a shorter way back via the Two Bridges Trail or continuing on the Queen's Garden Trail to Sunrise Point. For the short version, allow at least an hour on this 1.3-mile trail, with 515 feet of elevation change. *Moderate.* ⊠ *Bryce Canyon National Park* ✛ *Trailhead: At Sunset Point.*

Peekaboo Loop

TRAIL | The reward of this steep trail is the Three Wise Men and Wall of Windows formations. Start at Bryce, Sunrise, or Sunset Point and allow four to five hours to hike the 5½-mile trail or 7-mile double-loop. Horses use this trail spring–fall and have the right-of-way. *Difficult.* ⊠ *Bryce Canyon National Park* ⊹ *Trailheads: Bryce, Sunset, or Sunrise Point.*

★ Queen's Garden Trail

TRAIL | **FAMILY** | This hike is the easiest way down into the amphitheater, with 450 feet of elevation change leading to a short tunnel, quirky hoodoos, and lots of like-minded hikers. It's the essential Bryce "sampler." Allow two hours total to hike the 1½-mile trail plus the ½-mile rim-side path and back. *Easy.* ⊠ *Bryce Canyon National Park* ⊹ *Trailhead: At Sunrise Point.*

★ Queen's/Navajo Combination Loop

TRAIL | **FAMILY** | By walking this extended 3-mile loop, you can get a clear sense of what makes this park so special; it takes a little more than two hours. The route passes fantastic formations and an open forest of pine and juniper on the amphitheater floor. Descend into the amphitheater from Sunrise Point on the Queen's Garden Trail and ascend via the Navajo Loop; return to your starting point via the Rim Trail. *Moderate.* ⊠ *Bryce Canyon National Park* ⊹ *Trailheads: At Sunset and Sunrise Points.*

★ Rim Trail

TRAIL | A 1-mile section of this level trail connects Sunrise and Sunset Points and is an ideal way to launch or wrap up your day. Take your time strolling. Evening is the best time for photos, as much of the rim looks out to the east over the amphitheater. Listen for songbirds, look for a silent swooping owl, and watch the sun's last rays dance on the hoodoos. This section of the trail is wheelchair accessible, and pets on leashes are welcome. More ambitious walkers can enjoy the full trail, which extends 5½ miles between Bryce Point and Fairyland Point—this longer trail does have some elevation changes. *Easy to moderate.* ⊠ *Main Park Rd., Bryce Canyon National Park* ⊹ *Trailhead: Just east of the Lodge at Bryce Canyon* ⊕ *www.nps.gov/brca/planyourvisit/rimtrail.htm.*

Tower Bridge

TRAIL | This relatively short but steep, less-crowded hike on the Fairyland Loop takes you to a natural bridge deep in the amphitheater. Walk through pink and white badlands with hoodoos all around on this 3-mile trip that takes two to three hours and incurs 760 feet of elevation change. *Moderate.* ⊠ *Bryce Canyon National Park* ⊹ *Trailhead: At Sunrise Point.*

The aptly named Wall of Windows is a highlight of the challenging Peekaboo Loop trail.

VISITOR CENTERS
★ Bryce Canyon Visitor Center
VISITOR CENTER | FAMILY | Even if you're eager to hit the hoodoos, the visitor center—just to your right after the park entrance station—is the best place to start if you want to know what you're looking at and how it got there. The exhibits are well-designed, and there's an excellent 24-minute film about the park. Rangers staff a counter where you can ask questions or let them map out an itinerary of "must-sees" based on your time and physical abilities. You can also use the Wi-Fi, pick up backcountry camping permits, and browse the books, maps, and other goods sold in the Bryce Canyon Natural History Association gift shop, whose proceeds help to support park programs and conservation. ⊠ Hwy. 63, Bryce Canyon National Park ☎ 435/834–5322 ⊕ www. nps.gov/brca.

🍴 Restaurants

★ The Lodge at Bryce Canyon Restaurant
$$ | AMERICAN | With a high-beam ceiling, tall windows, and a massive stone fireplace, the dining room at this historic lodge set among towering pines abounds with rustic western charm. The kitchen serves three meals a day (reservations aren't accepted, so be prepared for a wait), and the dishes—highlights of which include elk chili, buffalo sirloin steak, pineapple-glazed roasted pork tenderloin, and almond-and-panko-crusted trout—feature organic or sustainable ingredients whenever possible. **Known for:**

Native American History in Bryce

According to Paiute legend, the hoodoos are Legend People, predecessors who were turned to stone by coyotes, some still with paint on their faces.

Human history in Bryce Canyon dates back some 2,000 years to the Ancestral Puebloans, also known as Anasazi. The Fremont people are believed to have lived in the area in the 1200s, followed by the Paiute. According to author Greer Chesher, who's written extensively about Bryce Canyon, the Paiutes depended on springs "in and around Bryce, like piki-pa below Yovimpa Point, which may be what we know today as Riggs Spring." In summer, the Fremont and Paiute cultures would have been attracted by the Bryce rim's pine nuts, sego lily roots, and animals for nourishment.

The 19th-century establishment of 11 Mormon settlements in southern Utah heralded the end of the Paiute relationship with the lands in and around Bryce. Not only did the tribe face competition for land and resources, but it also faced epidemics. Many Paiute lives were lost to disease at this time. Later in the century, those who survived were moved to reservations. They eventually lost not only these lands but also, in the 1950s, their designation as a tribe owing to federal government policies of the time. Even basic health care became an issue: between 1954 and 1980, more than half of the remaining Paiute died. Although recognition of the Paiute as a tribe was restored in 1980, only a fraction of their original lands was returned to them.

good selection of local craft beers; delicious desserts, including a fudge-brownie sundae and six-layer carrot cake; hearty breakfasts. $ Average main: $29 ⊠ Bryce Canyon National Park ✛ Off Main Park Rd. ☎ 435/834–8700 ⊕ www.visitbrycecanyon.com ⊗ Closed Nov.–Mar.

Valhalla Pizzeria and Coffee Shop

$ | PIZZA | FAMILY | A quick and casual 40-seat eatery across the parking lot from the Lodge at Bryce Canyon, this pizzeria and coffee shop is a good bet for an inexpensive meal, especially when the lodge dining room is too crowded. Coffee shop choices include an espresso bar, house-made pastries, and fresh fruit, or kick back on the tranquil patio in the evening and enjoy fresh pizza or salad. **Known for:** convenient and casual; decent beer and wine selection; filling pizzas. $ Average main: $15 ⊠ Bryce Canyon National Park ✛ Off Main Park Rd. ☎ 435/834–8709 ⊕ www. visitbrycecanyon.com ⊗ Closed mid-Sept.–mid-May.

🏨 Hotels

★ The Lodge at Bryce Canyon

$$ | HOTEL | This historic, rugged stone-and-wood lodge close to the amphitheater's rim offers western-inspired rooms with semiprivate balconies or porches in two motel-style buildings; suites in the historic inn; and cozy, beautifully designed lodgepole pine-and-stone cabins, some with cathedral ceilings and gas fireplaces. **Pros:** steps from canyon rim and trails; lodge is steeped in history and has loads of personality; cabins have fireplaces and exude rustic charm. **Cons:** closed in winter; books up fast; no TVs or air-conditioning. ⑤ *Rooms from: $254* ⊠ *Bryce Canyon National Park* ✛ *Off Main Park Rd.* ☎ *435/834–8700, 855/765–0255* ⊕ *www.visitbrycecanyon.com* ⊗ *Closed Nov.–Mar.* 🛏 *113 rooms* ❀❀ *No Meals.*

🛍 Shopping

Bryce Canyon General Store

GENERAL STORE | Buy groceries, T-shirts, hats, books, postcards, and camping items that you might have left behind, as well as snacks, drinks, juices, and quick to-go meals at this handy variety store between Sunrise Point and North Campground. Picnic tables under pine trees offer a shady spot to dine al fresco. ⊠ *Bryce Canyon National Park* ✛ *Off Main Park Rd.* ⊕ *www.visitbrycecanyon. com* ⊗ *Closed Nov.–Mar.*

The Lodge at Bryce Canyon Gift Shop

CRAFTS | Here you can buy Native American and Southwestern crafts, such as pottery and jewelry, along with T-shirts, light outdoor apparel, dolls, and books. ⊠ *Bryce Canyon National Park* ✛ *Off Main Park Rd.* ☎ *435/834–8700* ⊕ *www.visitbrycecanyon. com* ⊗ *Closed Nov.–Mar.*

Visitor Center Bookstore

BOOKS | The Bryce Canyon Natural History Association runs a bookstore inside the park visitor center where you can find maps, books, videos, stuffed animals, clothing, and postcards. ⊠ *Hwy. 63, Bryce Canyon National Park* ☎ *888/362–2642* ⊕ *www.bryce-canyon.org.*

Under-the-Rim

Bryce Canyon's longest trail leads backpackers under the rim of the park's plateau, which edges the natural amphitheater. Hiking the full 23-mile Under-the-Rim Trail will require an overnight stay,

but you can tackle shorter sections of it via a few different connecting trails accessed from overlooks along the main park road. On clear nights, the stargazing can be stellar.

◉ Sights

SCENIC STOPS

Agua Canyon

VIEWPOINT | This overlook in the southern section of the park has a nice view of several standout hoodoos. Look for the top-heavy formation called The Hunter, which actually has a few small hardy trees growing on its cap. As the rock erodes, the park evolves; snap a picture because The Hunter may look different the next time you visit. ⊠ *Main Park Rd.*

★ Natural Bridge

VIEWPOINT | Formed over millions of years by wind, water, and chemical erosion, this 85-foot-tall, rusty-orange arch formation—one of several rock arches in the park—is an essential photo op from one of the more popular overlooks on the park's scenic drive. Beyond the parking lot lies a rare stand of aspen trees, their leaves twinkling in the wind. Watch out for distracted drivers at this stunning viewpoint. ⊠ *Main Park Rd.*

Paria View

VIEWPOINT | Gaze into the Paria River watershed below at one of the park's only southwest-facing overlooks. Far below you, hardy hikers on the Under-the-Rim Trail may be refilling their supplies at the lush, green Yellow Creek meadow. Also, look for mule deer, elk, and pronghorn in the meadows near here—and peregrine falcons nesting or hunting along the cliffs. Skiers love the 3½-mile cross-country loop accessed from this point in winter. ⊠ *Bryce Canyon National Park ⊹ Off Bryce Point Rd.*

Piracy Point

VIEWPOINT | Offering an impressive range of panoramas, this peaceful overlook that's popular for picnicking lies ¼ mile north of Farview Point (to which it's connected by an easy trail), slightly off the main road. ⊠ *Off Main Park Rd.*

TRAILS

The Hat Shop Trail

TRAIL | The sedimentary haberdashery sits 2 miles from the trailhead at Bryce Point. Hard gray caps balance precariously atop narrow pedestals of softer, rust-color rock. Allow three to four hours to travel this somewhat strenuous—there's a 1,380-foot elevation gain—but rewarding 4-mile round-trip trek that's part of the

Although short (1½ miles), the "easiest" route down into the amphitheater takes two hours.

northernmost section of the longer Under-the-Rim Trail. *Moderate–Difficult.* ✛ *Trailhead: Bryce Point.*

★ Under-the-Rim Trail

TRAIL | Starting at Bryce Point, the trail travels 23 miles to Rainbow Point, passing through The Pink Cliffs, traversing Agua Canyon and Ponderosa Canyon, and taking you by several springs. Most of the hike is on the amphitheater floor, characterized by up-and-down terrain among stands of ponderosa pine; the elevation change totals about 4,500 feet. It's the park's longest trail, but four trailheads along the main park road allow you to connect to the Under-the-Rim Trail and cover its length as a series of day hikes. ⚠ **The connecting Agua Canyon Trail from Ponderosa Point was closed indefinitely due to storm damage in 2023; check with the visitor center and/or the current conditions section of the park website before you visit to find out if it has reopened.** Allow at least two days to hike the route in its entirety, and although it's not a hoodoo-heavy hike, there's plenty to see to make it a more leisurely three-day affair. Those camping along the trail must obtain a backcountry permit from the visitor center before they set out. *Difficult.* ✛ *Trailheads: At Bryce Point, Swamp Canyon, Ponderosa Canyon (closed for renovations), and Rainbow Point* ⊕ *www.nps.gov/brca/planyourvisit/backcountryinfo.htm.*

Rainbow and Yovimpa Points

Heading south from the park entrance, this serene patch of wilderness with an elevation of around 9,000 lies at the very end of the 18-mile park road. The area includes an easy 1-mile trail through a forest of bristlecone pines as well the much more rigorous 8.8-mile Riggs Spring Loop Trail. The viewpoints at Rainbow and Yovimpa look to the north and south, so you'll want to visit both. One popular strategy, especially if it's your first time visiting the park, is to drive directly to this point, and then visit the many overlooks along the route as you make your way back north toward the Bryce Amphitheater.

◉ Sights

PICNIC AREAS

Yovimpa Point Picnic Area

NATURE SIGHT | At the southern end of the park's scenic drive, this shady, quiet spot looks out onto the 100-mile vistas from the rim. Arguably the prettiest picnic spot in the park, it has tables and restrooms. ⊠ *End of Main Park Rd., Bryce Canyon National Park*

SCENIC STOPS

★ Rainbow and Yovimpa Points

VIEWPOINT | Just a half-mile apart, Rainbow and Yovimpa Points offer two spectacular panoramas facing opposite directions. Rainbow Point's best view is to the north overlooking the southern rim of the amphitheater and giving a glimpse of Grand Staircase–Escalante National Monument; Yovimpa Point's vista spreads out to the south. On an especially clear day you can see all the way to Arizona's highest point, Humphreys Peak, 150 miles away. Yovimpa Point also has a shady and quiet picnic area with tables and restrooms. You can hike between them on the easy Bristlecone Loop or tackle the more strenuous 8.8-mile Riggs Spring Loop Trail, which passes the tallest point in the park. ⊠ *End of Main Park Rd., 18 miles south of park entrance.*

TRAILS

Bristlecone Loop

TRAIL | This 1-mile trail with a modest 200 feet of elevation gain lets you see the park from its highest points of more than 9,000 feet, alternating between spruce and fir forest and wide-open vistas out over Grand Staircase–Escalante National Monument and beyond. You might see yellow-bellied marmots and dusky grouse, critters not typically found at lower elevations in the park. Allow about an hour. *Easy.* ⊹ *Trailhead: At Rainbow Point parking lot.*

Riggs Spring Loop Trail

TRAIL | One of the park's two true backpacker trails, this rigorous 8.8-mile path has overnight options at three campsites along the way. You'll journey past groves of twinkling aspen trees and the eponymous spring close to the campsite. Start at either Yovimpa or Rainbow Point and be prepared for 1,500 feet of elevation change. Campers need to check in at the visitor center ahead of time to obtain a backcountry permit. *Difficult.* ⊠ *Bryce Canyon National Park* ⚓ *Trailheads: At Yovimpa and Rainbow Points, 18 miles south of park entrance.*

Activities

Bryce Canyon's myriad hiking trails offer a rewarding way to get a sense of the park's singular landscape. At these elevations, you should prepare to stop and catch your breath regularly. It gets warm in summer but usually not too uncomfortably hot, so hiking farther into the depths of the park isn't difficult. Just take care to choose a hike that's within your abilities.

Air Excursions

Bryce Canyon Airlines & Helicopters

AIR EXCURSIONS | For a bird's-eye view of Bryce Canyon National Park, take a dramatic helicopter ride or airplane tour over the fantastic sandstone formations. Longer full-canyon tours and added excursions to sites such as the Grand Canyon, Monument Valley, Lake Powell, and Zion are also offered. Flights last from 35 minutes to four hours. ⊠ *Bryce Canyon National Park* ☎ *435/834–8060* ⊕ *www.rubysinn.com/scenic-flights* ✈ *From $165.*

Biking

Bikes are permitted in the park only on park roads and paved shared-use paths, not on any unpaved trails. Cycling the park's entire scenic road from Bryce Canyon City to Rainbow Point—about 20 miles each way—isn't the easiest 40 miles you will have ever pedaled, but it's a great workout with plenty of opportunities to stop and take in phenomenal views. You'll contend with some traffic, especially in high season, but less so early in the day. The elevation gain from north to south is only about 1,200 feet, but since you're starting at nearly 8,000 feet above sea level, your body may really feel it. For an easier go, you could ride the free park shuttle (it accommodates up to two bikes) to Rainbow Point

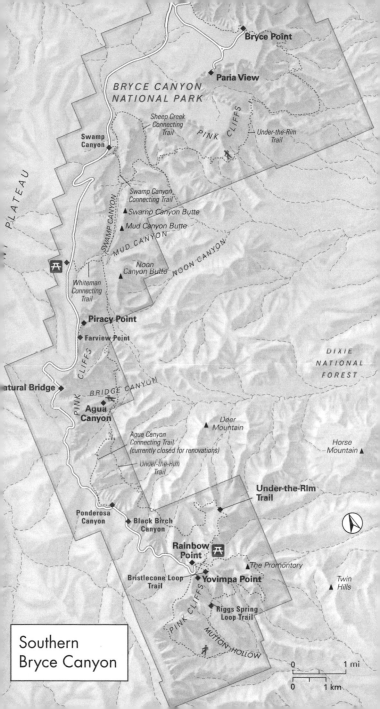

Southern
Bryce Canyon

and bike back to the entrance, a one-way trip that's steadily down-hill. Another less-taxing option is to rent an e-bike.

Mountain bike or hybrid riders can tackle the local span of the Great Western Trail, which spans the Rockies for some 4,455 miles from Mexico to Canada—a portion of it bisects Highway 63 between Bryce Canyon City and the Fairyland Point turn-out. It's open to bikes, four-wheelers, horses, and (in winter) snowmobiles.

Bryce Canyon EZ Riders Electric Bike Rentals

BIKING | This outfitter on the edge of Bryce Canyon City rents a variety of state-of-the-art e-bikes; rates are $40 for two hours, $60 for a half-day, and $100 for a full day. ⊠ *450 Airport Rd., Bryce Canyon National Park* ☎ *435/690–9520* ⊕ *www.brycecanyonezriders.com* ⧉ *From $40.*

Ruby's Inn Bike Rentals

BIKING | Ruby's Inn rents mountain bikes for $35 per half-day and $50 for a full-day. The shop can also recommend and provide a shuttle service ($40 one-way or $60 round-trip) to single-track trails in the surrounding region (bikes are not allowed off-road in the park). They also rent e-bikes for $65 per half-day. ⊠ *110 Center St., Bryce Canyon National Park* ☎ *435/834–8032* ⊕ *www.rubysinn.com/mountain-bike-rentals* ⧉ *From $35.*

Bird-Watching

More than 210 bird species have been identified in Bryce. Violet-green swallows and white-throated swifts are common, as are Steller's jays, American coots, rufous hummingbirds, and mountain bluebirds. Lucky bird-watchers may see golden eagles floating across the skies above the pink rocks of the amphitheater, and if you look closely you might spot an osprey nest high in the canyon wall. The best time in the park for avian variety is May through July.

Camping

The two campgrounds in Bryce Canyon are family-friendly and drive-in. Additionally, there are a handful of backcountry sites only used by intrepid overnight hikers. North Campground operates on a reservation system in high season; the rest of the year, it's first-come, first-served, as is the case with Sunset Campground. Slots fill up fast, particularly in summer, so book ahead when you can. The nightly rates are $20 for tent sites and $30 for RV sites. Most

Yovimpa Point Overlook has a shady picnic area and 100-mile vistas.

of the park's campsites are closed in winter, but one loop of North Campground remains open year-round.

You'll also find camping facilities at most nearby state parks (including Coral Pink Sand Dunes, Kodachrome Basin, and Escalante Petrified Forest), at Cedar Breaks National Monument, and in many areas within the Dixie National Forest. There are also several upscale glamping operations within an hour or two of the park.

IN THE PARK

North Campground. This cool, shady retreat in a forest of ponderosa pines is close to the overlooks of Bryce Amphitheater as well as the general store, the Lodge at Bryce Canyon, and the visitor center. Just be aware that some sites feel crowded and not very private. From mid-May through early October, sites are available by reservation; the rest of the year, they're first-come, first-served. ✛ *Main park road, ½ mile south of visitor center* ☎ *435/834–5322* ⊕ *www.recreation.gov* ⌨ *50 RV sites, 46 tent sites.*

Sunset Campground. This serene, alpine campground is across the main park road from the Lodge at Bryce Canyon and about a 10- to 15-minute walk from the overlooks and trailheads along the rim in Bryce Amphitheater. The campground is generally open mid-April through October, and sites are available first-come, first-served. ✛ *Main park road, 2 miles south of visitor center* ☎ *435/834–5322* ⌨ *50 RV sites, 50 tent sites.*

OUTSIDE THE PARK

Bryce Canyon Pines Campground and RV Park. This campground 7 miles from the park entrance is shady and quiet. It's adjacent to the Bryce Canyon Pines Lodge motel and restaurant and has showers and a guest laundry. ⚓ *Hwy. 12, Bryce Canyon City* ☎ *435/834–5441* ⊕ *bcpines.com* ⏪ *15 tent sites, 30 RV sites, 1 group site.*

Ruby's Inn Campground and RV Park. Just a mile north of the park entrance, this large campground spreads out a few steps from the Ruby's complex. Most of the campsites are in an open area, with full hook-ups or electricity and water; there are also tent sites, group camping sites, and rustic tepees and cabins beneath the pine and fir trees that surround the RV park. The campground has plenty of amenities, including a seasonal outdoor pool, laundry facilities, and showers. ⚓ *300 S. Main St., Bryce Canyon City* ☎ *866/878–9373, 435/834–5341* ⊕ *www.brycecanyoncampgrounds.com* ⏪ *250 sites.*

Educational Programs

RANGER PROGRAMS

You can learn more about the following programs on the park website: ⊕ *www.nps.gov/brca/planyourvisit/ranger-programs.htm*

Evening Programs. Bryce Canyon's natural diversity comes alive during ranger talks and multimedia programs held late May through early September in the auditorium of the Lodge at Bryce Canyon. These talks touch on geology, astronomy, wildlife, history, and many other topics related to Bryce Canyon and the West.

Geology Talks. Rangers host free 20-to 30-minute discussions at 11 am year-round about the long geological history of Bryce Canyon. These interesting talks are held at Sunset Point.

Junior Ranger Program. Kids can pick up a free program booklet at the visitor center or download it online. They then have to complete several fun and easy activities to earn a badge. ⊕ *www.nps. gov/brca/learn/kidsyouth/beajuniorranger.htm*

Telescopes Program. You can see vast arrays of stars amid the dark, generally clear skies in these parts. Learn what you're viewing during one of these engaging 75-minute talks and telescope-viewing sessions held around 9:30 pm on Friday and Saturday (late May–early Sept.) in the visitor center. Reservations are required and can be made at the visitor center the day of the event—it's best to reserve in the morning.

Hiking

There's a pattern to most hikes in Bryce—start at the rim, descend into the canyon, and explore among the red rocks before climbing back out. Having to ascend to the rim at the end can make even shorter jaunts in the park a bit strenuous—start with a short hike if you're new to hiking or unused to the altitude, and always pack extra water and allow plenty of time to complete—at least a half-day—your adventure before it gets dark. All the travels into the canyon can be steep and uneven in places, so always wear sturdy hiking boots. And be aware that bathrooms are at most trailheads but not down in the amphitheater. In summer, consider hiking in the morning to avoid the day's warmest temperatures and strongest sun. As long as you pace yourself, you're likely to have a marvelous time.

Utah Prairie Dog 👁

Bryce Canyon National Park reintroduced the Utah prairie dog (*Cynomys parvidens*) to its meadows during the 1970s and '80s. Numbering approximately 600 in Bryce today (and less than 10,000 across the southwestern portion of the state), the Utah prairie dog was initially protected under the Endangered Species Act in 1973, with its status improving slightly from "endangered" to "threatened" a decade later. Bryce is the only National Park Service unit where these creatures are found.

If you have time for just one trail, choose the Queen's Garden/ Navajo combination loop. With a little more time, pick one of the outlying hikes: the Fairyland Loop, The Hat Shop Trail, or the Riggs Springs Loop Trail (which has backcountry campsites, but at 8.8 miles can be tackled in one long day).

One of the smaller U.S. national parks by area, Bryce Canyon does not have as much backcountry as, say, the Grand Canyon or Zion. The 23-mile Under-the-Rim Trail is the primary backcountry option. Situated almost entirely at the base of the canyon, it is a rugged environment where hikers do need to pay attention to trail markers and maps and watch for wildlife. Allow at least two and ideally three days to hike the length of the trail in either direction. For a shorter experience, drop down to the trail via any of four connecting paths (perhaps Swamp Canyon or Whiteman Bench) along the park road. You'll need to arrange a pickup or drop-off, as the park shuttle service doesn't go beyond the road to Bryce Point.

Horseback Riding

Few activities conjure up the Old West like riding a horse, and Bryce Canyon offers a wonderful opportunity to see a remarkable landscape from the saddle. Many of the park's hiking trails were first formed beneath the hooves of cattle wranglers, and their modern-day counterparts now guide tourists over these and other trails. Canyon Trail Rides is the park's designated outfitter.

Canyon Trail Rides

HORSEBACK RIDING | **FAMILY** | Descend to the floor of the Bryce Canyon Amphitheater via horse or mule—many visitors have no riding experience, so don't hesitate to join in. A two-hour ride (children as young as seven can participate) ambles along the amphitheater floor through Queen's Garden before returning to Sunrise Point. The three-hour expedition (children must be at least 10 years old) follows the Peekaboo Loop, winds past Fairyland, and passes The Wall of Windows before returning to Sunrise Point. Two rides a day of each type leave in the morning and early afternoon. Rides are offered April–October. ✉ *Lodge at Bryce Canyon, Off Hwy. 63, Bryce Canyon National Park* ☎ *435/679–8665* ⊕ *www.canyon-rides.com* 🍴 *From $75.*

Winter Activities

Unlike most of Utah's other national parks, Bryce Canyon receives plenty of snow, making it a popular cross-country ski area. The Rim Trail, Paria Loop, and other paths above the canyon are popular destinations. While skiing into the canyon is not permitted, you can snowshoe on any of the park's trails, and ranger-led snowshoe treks lasting about two hours are offered in winter. The visitor center sells shoe-traction devices to assist with hiking in icy or snowy conditions, and you can rent snowshoes and cross-country skis just outside the park at Ruby's Inn.

Ruby's Winter Activities Center

SKIING & SNOWBOARDING | **FAMILY** | This facility just outside the park rents snowshoes and cross-country ski equipment and grooms miles of private, no-cost trails that connect to the ungroomed trails inside the park. They also operate an ice-skating ribbon and rent skates. ✉ *110 Center St., Bryce Canyon National Park* ☎ *435/834–5341, 866/866–6616* ⊕ *www.rubysinn.com/winter-activities.*

Chapter 6

BRYCE CANYON GATEWAYS

Updated by
Andrew Collins

⊙ Sights   🍴 Restaurants   🛏 Hotels   🛍 Shopping   🍸 Nightlife

★★★★★   ★★★★☆   ★★★★☆   ★★★☆☆   ★★★☆☆

WELCOME TO BRYCE CANYON GATEWAYS

TOP REASONS TO GO

★ **A wild ride:** Spectacular Highway 12 snakes its way to Grand Staircase–Escalante National Monument.

★ **Shakespeare on high:** Watch plays by The Bard during Cedar City's Utah Shakespeare Festival.

★ **Epic stargazing:** Cedar Breaks National Monument has become a center of astro-tourism.

1 Bryce Canyon City. Just north of and en route to Bryce Canyon, this touristy town has the nearest travel services to the park, including basic motels and restaurants, a gas station, and parking for the free park shuttle.

2 Panguitch. Count on this low-key town for inexpensive, casual lodgings and eateries within striking distance of Bryce Canyon and Cedar Breaks.

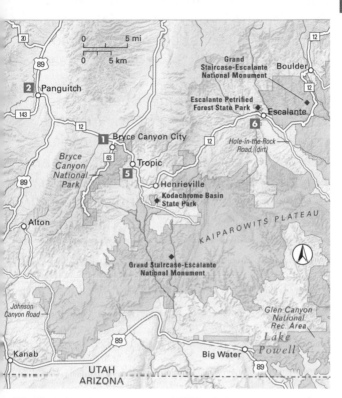

3 Brian Head. The state's southernmost ski town is the nearest base for exploring Cedar Breaks.

4 Cedar City. The home of Southern Utah University has many cultural draws, including the Utah Shakespeare Festival.

5 Tropic. Tiny and cute Tropic has several good restaurants and lodgings and is handy for visiting Bryce Canyon.

6 Escalante. This picturesque village on Highway 12 is a recreation hub with an appealing mix of places to stay and eat.

Several cool—literally, given the altitude, and figuratively—towns make great bases for exploring Bryce Canyon National Park. To the west are Panguitch, a pioneer town; the small ski town of Brian Head; and Cedar City, home to a university and a renowned summer Shakespeare festival. Just outside the park entrance, the unfortunately heavily commercialized town of Bryce Canyon City contains the nearest travel services to the park. Just to the east is tiny Tropic, and another 40 miles east is Escalante.

Both Panguitch and Brian Head are also ideal bases for exploring Cedar Breaks National Monument, an International Dark Sky Park that presents occasional astronomy programs. Set at 10,000 feet, in cold months, Cedar Breaks is generally accessible only by snowshoes, skis, and snowmobiles. Likewise, some of the services in Panguitch close seasonally—at an elevation of over 6,600 feet, winters here are snowy. In fact, during the harsh winter of 1864, pioneers facing food shortages sent a rescue party to another town for help. The group couldn't navigate its wagons through the deep snow, so its members ventured forth on foot, discovering that by laying their quilts down on the snow, they could walk without sinking. The event is commemorated at the town's annual Quilt Walk Festival.

Winter is prime time in Brian Head, one of Utah's highest-altitude ski resorts. Less crowded than bigger resorts to the north, it's known for its dry-powder skiing and, in warmer months, its mountain biking and hiking.

With good restaurants, reliable lodging, and interesting museums, Cedar City is a handy overnight base for both Bryce Canyon and Zion national parks. The community is energized by students at Southern Utah University, which, in the 1960s, established the acclaimed Utah Shakespeare Festival—a major draw throughout the summer.

Bryce Canyon City is tiny and has a few places to stay, eat, and pick up supplies, although prices tend to be steep for what's offered. Although the town of Tropic is also compact, it sits right outside Bryce Canyon National Park's eastern edge and has some great little dining and lodging options. Farther east of Bryce is Escalante, the gateway to the Grand Staircase–Escalante National Monument and an excellent place to stay if you're continuing north to Capitol Reef National Park. Some exciting, scenic routes lace the area, including the Hole-in-the-Rock Road, where four-wheel drive is recommended, and Highway 12 Scenic Byway.

Planning

Hotels

Cedar City and Escalante have the best selection of modern lodgings with comfortable amenities. You'll find a handful of lodgings near the ski slopes of Brian Head and also a few properties in the small towns of Tropic, Panguitch, and Bryce Canyon City. Several upscale glamping compounds have also opened throughout the region in recent years.

Restaurants

Hearty, down-to-earth fare is the norm in restaurants throughout the region, although a handful of more sophisticated spots specializing in contemporary, often globally inspired fare thrive in Cedar City. Note that some establishments don't serve alcohol and are closed on Sunday. A few also close seasonally.

⇨ *Hotel and restaurant reviews have been shortened. For full information visit Fodors.com. Restaurant prices are the average cost of a main course at dinner, or if dinner is not served, at lunch. Hotel prices are the lowest cost of a standard double room in high season.*

What It Costs			
$	$$	$$$	$$$$
RESTAURANTS			
under $20	$20–$30	$31–$40	over $40
HOTELS			
under $200	$200–$350	$351–$500	over $500

Bryce Canyon City

Right outside the park, this cluster of generally unremarkable lodging and dining options, shops, and travel services is handy if marred by excessive and touristy signage. But it does offer close proximity to Bryce Canyon, and it's where you pick up the free shuttle bus into the park.

GETTING HERE AND AROUND

Highway 63 passes right through town on the way to Bryce Canyon National Park's entrance, which is less than a mile south. The park's shuttle bus stops at several points in town.

Sights

MUSEUMS

Bryce Wildlife Adventure

SCIENCE MUSEUM | FAMILY | Imagine a zoo frozen in time: this 14,000-square-foot private museum contains more than 1,600 butterflies and 1,100 taxidermy animals in tableaux mimicking actual terrain and animal behavior. The animals and birds come from all parts of the world. An African room has baboons, bush pigs, Cape buffalo, and a lion. There's also a collection of about 40 living fallow deer that kids delight in feeding and ATV and bike rentals for touring scenic Highway 12 and the Paunsaugunt Plateau. ⊠ *1945 W. Hwy. 12, Bryce Canyon City* ☎ *435/834–5555* ⊕ *www.brycewildlifeadventure.com* ⌲ *$8* ⊗ *Closed Nov.–Mar.*

Restaurants

Bryce Canyon Pines Restaurant

$ | AMERICAN | FAMILY | Inside the Bryce Canyon Pines Lodge motel, about 5 miles northwest of Bryce Canyon City, this down-home, family-friendly roadhouse decorated with Old West photos and memorabilia serves reliably good stick-to-your-ribs breakfasts, hefty elk burgers, rib-eye steaks, and Utah rainbow trout. But the top draw here is homemade pie, which comes in a vast assortment of flavors, from banana-blueberry cream to boysenberry. **Known for:** delectable pies; convenient Highway 12 location; plenty of kids' options. $ *Average main: $17* ⊠ *2476 W. Hwy. 12, Bryce Canyon City* ☎ *435/834–5441* ⊕ *www.bcpines.com/ bryce-restaurant.*

Hotels

Best Western Plus Bryce Canyon Grand Hotel

$$$ | HOTEL | If you appreciate creature comforts but can do without much in the way of local personality, this four-story hotel just outside the park fits the bill—rooms are quite comfortable, with plush bedding, spacious bathrooms, and modern appliances, and there's an outdoor pool and pleasant patio. **Pros:** clean, spacious rooms; attractive pool; short drive or free shuttle ride from Bryce Canyon. **Cons:** the closest restaurants aren't very good; pricey for this chain; standard chain ambience. ⑤ *Rooms from: $409* ✉ *30 N. 100 E, Bryce Canyon City* ☎ *866/866–6634, 435/834–5700* ⊕ *www.brycecanyongrand.com* ⌥ *164 rooms* ⎮◎⎮ *Free Breakfast.*

Bryce Canyon Pines

$ | MOTEL | Most rooms in this motel in the sweeping high desert 6 miles southwest of the park entrance and close to Red Canyon have pleasant views of the surrounding pine trees and the mountains in the distance. **Pros:** guided horseback rides through Red Canyon; outdoor pool and hot tub; lively restaurant famed for homemade pies. **Cons:** thin walls; no shuttle bus to the park; furnishings are a bit dated. ⑤ *Rooms from: $153* ✉ *2476 Hwy. 12, Bryce Canyon City* ☎ *435/834–5441* ⊕ *www.bcpines.com* ⌥ *45 units* ⎮◎⎮ *No Meals.*

Under Canvas Bryce Canyon

$$$ | RESORT | FAMILY | This beautifully situated outpost of the popular Under Canvas luxury glamping brand in a juniper forest outside Widtsoe, a hiccup of a village about 15 miles north of the national park entrance, offers safari-chic canvas tents decked out with tasteful West Elm furnishings, private baths with eco-friendly products, and USB battery packs to keep your toys charged, plus a restaurant serving locally sourced breakfast and dinner fare. **Pros:** secluded and stunning setting on 750 high-desert acres; nightly campfires with complimentary s'mores; lots of activities— yoga, live music. **Cons:** relatively short season; a 20-minute drive from the park and area restaurants; on-site food options are limited and pricey. ⑤ *Rooms from: $359* ✉ *1325 S. Johns Valley Rd.* ☎ *888/496–1148* ⊕ *www.undercanvas.com/camps/bryce-canyon* ⊘ *Closed Oct.–early May* ⌥ *50 tents* ⎮◎⎮ *No Meals.*

⬤ Shopping

Ruby's Inn General Store

GENERAL STORE | On a busy evening, this giant mercantile bustles with tourists picking through souvenirs that range from sweatshirts to wind chimes. There's also Western wear, children's toys,

Along scenic Highway 12, Red Canyon has several easy-to-access trails.

holiday gifts, and groceries (albeit with pretty high prices), plus camping. Need a folding stove, sleeping bag, or fishing gear? You'll find it at Ruby's. You can also cross Main Street to where this ever-expanding complex has added a line of shops trimmed like an Old West town, complete with candy store and rock shop. ⊠ *26 S. Main St., Bryce Canyon City* ☎ *435/834–5484* ⊕ *www. rubysinn.com/rubys-inn-store.*

Panguitch

24 miles northwest of Bryce Canyon National Park.

An elevation of 6,650 feet keeps this town and its 1,750 residents cool. Main Street is lined with several distinctive brick late-19th-century buildings. A few inexpensive, mostly motel-style lodgings and a location midway between Bryce Canyon and Cedar Breaks National Monument make this a popular, economical launching pad for recreation in the area.

GETTING HERE AND AROUND

Panguitch is along one of the region's prettiest main thoroughfares, U.S. 89, and is also near the starting point of scenic Highway 12, which leads to Bryce Canyon and Grand Staircase–Escalante.

◉ Sights

★ Red Canyon

CANYON | This arresting 7,400-foot-elevation landscape of dark green ponderosa pines and Douglas fir trees is part of the Dixie National Forest. You'll see fiery-red sandstone pinnacles and hoodoos, as well as clear blue sky, as you make your way via Highway 12 from Panguitch to Bryce Canyon—at one point the road even passes beneath a dramatic red rock arch. Have a picnic and take a short stroll on one of the several trails that lead from the Red Canyon Visitor Center (open daily, late May to early September). Longer treks—the Hoodoo Loop, Pink Ledges, and Losee Canyon Trails all showcase the rewarding scenery—are worth checking out if you have a bit more time. Some trails are well-suited to mountain biking, horseback riding, and cross-country skiing, and the paved 5-mile Red Canyon Trail is ideal for road biking. There's also a campground. ⊠ *5375 Hwy. 12, Panguitch* ☎ *435/676–2676* ⊕ *www.fs.usda.gov/recarea/dixie/recarea/?recid=24942.*

🍴 Restaurants

Burger Barn

$ | **BURGER** | **FAMILY** | Order at the window and snag an outdoor table at this laid-back burger joint in a little red barn near Panguitch Lake, a great option en route to Cedar Breaks National Monument or Cedar City. The one-third-pound Black Angus steak burgers here come with a variety of toppings (bacon, onion rings), and the menu also has barbecue choices, such as pulled pork or beef brisket sandwiches, fish-and-chips, sweet-potato fries, and shakes and ice cream. **Known for:** giant burgers and smoked meats; pretty setting near an alpine lake; ice cream sundaes. ⑤ *Average main: $9* ⊠ *75 S. Hwy. 143, Panguitch* ☎ *435/676–2445* ⊕ *www.facebook.com/panguitchlakeutah* ⊗ *Closed mid-Sept.–mid–May.*

Cowboy's Smokehouse Cafe

$$ | **BARBECUE** | From the Western-style interior and creaky floors to the smoker out back, this rustic café has an aura of Texan authenticity—there are cowboy collectibles and game trophies lining the walls. No surprise that barbecue is the specialty here, and the restaurant has its own house-made sauce, with ample portions of favorites, such as ribs, mesquite-flavored beef, and pulled pork, along with lighter sandwiches and salads. **Known for:** German sausage platter; prodigious steaks; delicious desserts, including fruit cobbler and pies. ⑤ *Average main: $25* ⊠ *95 N. Main St., Panguitch* ☎ *435/676–8030* ⊕ *www.thecowboysmokehouse.com* ⊟ *No credit cards* ⊗ *Closed Sun. and late Nov.–mid-Mar.*

Hotels

Church's Blue Pine Motel

$ | MOTEL | This single-story 1930s-era motel in Panguitch's cute historic district doesn't look like much from the outside, but the rooms are clean, have refrigerators and microwaves, and are among the most affordable within striking distance of Bryce, Zion, and Cedar Breaks. **Pros:** you can pull your car right up to your room; in the center of town; rock-bottom rates. **Cons:** walls are a bit thin; very basic furnishings; not a lot to do right in Panguitch. ⑤ *Rooms from: $89* ⊠ *130 N. Main St., Panguitch* ☎ *435/676–8197, 800/299–6115* ⊕ *www.bluepinemotel.com* ⇨ *20 rooms* ⑩ *No Meals.*

★ Cottonwood Meadow Lodge

$$ | B&B/INN | Set in a sweeping valley along the main road between Panguitch and Hatch, this sweet and secluded 50-acre ranch comprises four roomy cottages decorated with stylish Western-style furnishings—leather sofas, indigenous artwork, bearskin rugs, handcarved beds and tables—and outfitted with well-equipped kitchens. **Pros:** peaceful, scenic setting; convenient to Bryce and Zion; self-catering and large sitting areas make rooms nice for families. **Cons:** few dining options nearby; no air-conditioning and no pets allowed; fills up well ahead on summer weekends. ⑤ *Rooms from: $224* ⊠ *U.S. 89, Mile marker 123, Panguitch* ☎ *435/676–8950* ⊕ *www.brycecanyoncabins.com* ⇨ *4 cabins* ⑩ *No Meals.*

Mountain Ridge Cabins and Lodging

$ | HOTEL | In the tiny village of Hatch, 15 miles south of Panguitch, you'll find this nicely maintained and reasonably priced campus of cozy cabins and standard hotel rooms, all of them spotlessly clean and attractively decorated with modern furnishings, large flat-screen TVs, refrigerators, microwaves, and high-quality bedding. **Pros:** you can park right in front of your room; within walking distance of a couple of restaurants; convenient for exploring Bryce and Zion. **Cons:** least expensive rooms are quite small; in a tiny town; on a slightly busy road. ⑤ *Rooms from: $119* ⊠ *106 S. Main St., Hatch* ☎ *435/735–4300, 877/877–9939* ⊕ *www.mountain-ridgelodging.com* ۞ *Closed Jan.–Apr.* ⇨ *24 rooms* ⑩ *No Meals.*

🛍 Shopping

Bryce Canyon Trading Post

CRAFTS | Near Red Canyon, a little east of U.S. 89, this rambling emporium carries high-quality Native American turquoise jewelry, beadwork, textiles, and other fine crafts, plus a number of souvenirs related to the nearby national parks. ✉ *2938 Hwy. 12, Panguitch* ☎ *435/676–2688*.

Brian Head

36 miles southwest of Panguitch.

This tiny town's Brian Head Resort is Utah's southernmost and highest ski area at well over 9,000 feet, but the area's summer recreation, especially mountain biking, has also developed energetically in recent years. There are now more than 200 miles of trails for bikers, many of which are served by chairlift or shuttle services. The bright red-orange rock formations of Cedar Breaks National Monument are several miles south of town.

The snow season is still the high season here, so book winter lodging in advance and expect higher room rates. During the fall "mud season" (October and November) and spring "slush season" (April and May), some local businesses shut down in this village with fewer than 100 year-round residents.

GETTING HERE AND AROUND

If coming from Panguitch, take Highway 143 west. From Cedar City, most of the year you take Highway 14 east to Highways 143 and 148 north. But in winter, when Highway 148 is closed, you'll need to take Interstate 15 north to Parowan and then Highway 143 south. Whichever way you arrive, the drive takes about the same amount of time (45 minutes to an hour) and is wonderfully scenic.

ⓤ Sights

Brian Head Peak Observation

SCENIC DRIVE | This 11,312-foot stone lookout hut was built by the Civilian Conservation Corps (CCC) in 1935 atop the highest summit in Iron County. You can see for miles in every direction, as far as Nevada and Arizona, enjoying especially dramatic views of nearby Cedar Breaks National Monument. The windy and dramatic, nearly 3-mile drive along bumpy and unpaved Forest Road 047 from Highway 143 (take it slowly) is part of the fun; when there's snow, the last section of road is closed to vehicles, but you can still hike or snowshoe up to the top. You can also hike to the summit from the junction of Rocky Road and Highway 143—the rugged and picturesque trek is about 3½ miles each way. ✉ *End of Forest Rd. 047, Brian Head* ☎ *435/865–3700* ⊕ *www.fs.usda. gov/recarea/dixie/recarea/?recid=24916*.

Many visitors "explore" Cedar Breaks National Monument from roadside overlooks, so its trails are often blissfully crowd-free.

★ Cedar Breaks National Monument

NATIONAL PARK | Cedar Breaks is a 3-mile-long natural amphitheater that plunges a half-mile into the Markagunt Plateau, offering spectacular scenery and fewer crowds than at the area's better known national parks. Mostly short alpine hiking trails trace the rim, meandering past wildflowers in summer. You can get a nice view of these distinctive red rock formations that bear a strong resemblance to those of Bryce Canyon at the handful of overlooks along Highway 148—which means hikers, skiers, and snowshoers can usually find solitude along the trails.

Winter is one of the best times to visit, when snow drapes the red-orange formations. A much-needed new visitor center with a park store, exhibits, a new restroom facility, and sheltered outdoor space for public programming is scheduled to open by the Sunset Trailhead parking area by spring 2024. From here, you can hike the 1-mile round-trip Sunset Trail, which is paved and wheelchair accessible, or embark on the most memorable of the park's hikes, the 5-mile round-trip South Rim Trail. This latter trek is moderately challenging, but if time is short, just hike the first mile to the Spectra Point viewpoint for an eye-popping panorama. Across Highway 148, the easy 0.6-mile round-trip Nature Trail connects with Point Supreme Campground, which has 25 tent and RV sites. In winter, call ahead for conditions (the road is sometimes closed due to heavy snowfall), and keep in mind that visitor facilities are closed from around October through late May, and sometimes longer if there's a lot of snow. ⊠ *Hwy. 148, Brian Head* ✛ *3½*

*miles north of Hwy. 14 ☎ 435/986–7120 ⊕ www.nps.gov/cebr
🗟 $10 per person (free under the age of 16) ⊗ Visitor center
closed mid-Oct.–late May.*

🛏 Hotels

Brian Head Lodge & Spa

$ | RESORT | FAMILY | With its stunning scenery and prime loca-
tion, this modern mission-style lodge is a welcoming base for
outdoor adventures and offers a number of amenities, including
a bar and grill, outdoor deck, indoor pool, and hot tubs, plus a
spa where you can enjoy a range of body and beauty treatments.
Pros: comfortable base for outdoor recreation; game room is
popular with families; mountain views. **Cons:** not directly on the
slopes; rooms lack kitchenettes; on-site restaurant gets mixed
reviews. *⑤ Rooms from: $99 ⊠ 314 Hunter Ridge Rd., Brian Head
☎ 435/691–8682 ⊕ www.brianhead.com ⇥ 112 rooms ⓘⓞⓘ Free
Breakfast.*

Cedar City

33 miles west of Brian Head.

Rich iron-ore deposits captured the attention of Mormon leader
Brigham Young. He ordered the establishment of a Church of
Jesus Christ of Latter-day Saints mission here in what is now
southwestern Utah's second largest community, with a population of about 41,400 (up from just 13,000 in 1990). The first
ironworks and foundry opened in 1851 and operated for only eight
years, problems with the furnace, flooding, and hostility between
settlers and regional Native Americans eventually put out the
flame. Residents then turned to ranching and farming for their
livelihoods, and Cedar City has thrived as an agricultural center
ever since.

Since the founding of Southern Utah University in 1897, the city
has been an educational and cultural hub as well. The university
campus hosts the community's most popular event: the Utah
Shakespeare Festival, whose season runs from late June through
October. This attractive, youthful gateway to both Zion and Bryce
Canyon national parks is also well situated for exploring the Brian
Head area and Cedar Breaks National Monument.

GETTING HERE AND AROUND

Interstate 15 cuts right through Cedar City. Though downtown is
walkable, you'll want a car to explore farther afield.

FESTIVALS

★ Utah Shakespeare Festival

THEATER | Since 1962, Cedar City has been Bard-crazy, staging productions of Shakespeare's plays from mid-June through mid-October in three Southern Utah University campus theaters, the largest of which is an open-air replica of Shakespeare's Globe Theatre. The Tony award–winning festival that has featured Jeremy Irons, Ty Burrell, and Bradley Whitford over the years also presents literary seminars, backstage tours, cabarets showcasing festival actors, and an outdoor preshow with Elizabethan performers. Try to book well in advance, as many performances sell out. ⊠ *195 W. Center St.* ☎ *435/586–7878, 800/752–9849* ⊕ *www.bard.org.*

Sights

Frontier Homestead State Park Museum

HISTORY MUSEUM | **FAMILY** | This interactive living-history museum devoted to the county's early iron industry is home to a number of interesting attractions, including a bullet-scarred stagecoach that ran in the days of Butch Cassidy and the oldest standing home in all of southern Utah, built in 1851. Local artisans demonstrate pioneer crafts, and numerous mining artifacts and tools are on display. ⊠ *585 N. Main St., Cedar City* ☎ *435/586–9290* ⊕ *www. frontierhomestead.org* ⊠ *$4* ⊗ *Closed Sun. in Sept.–Apr.*

IG Winery

WINERY | In a state with few wineries, this popular operation in downtown Cedar City sources grapes from respected vineyards in California's Napa and Sonoma Valleys, Washington's Columbia Valley, and Oregon's Rogue Valley. The Bordeaux-style reds are well-crafted, though spendy, while more moderately priced Tempranillo and Sangiovese also have plenty of fans. With exposed brick walls and hardwood floors, the handsome tasting room is hung with local art and warmed by a fireplace in winter. There's also a sunny patio, and live bands perform regularly. ⊠ *59 W. Center St.* ☎ *435/867–9463* ⊕ *www.igwinery.com* ⊗ *Closed Mon.*

Southern Utah Museum of Art (SUMA)

ART MUSEUM | Set in a striking modern building that opened in 2016 and was designed to resemble the region's canyons and rock formations, this excellent regional art museum with a peaceful sculpture garden is part of Southern Utah University's cultural compound, along with the Utah Shakespeare Festival theaters. The galleries feature selections from the museum's permanent collection of some 2,000 works—including pieces by Renoir, Dalí, Picasso, and Thomas Hart Benton—along with rotating shows that shine a light on emerging regional artists as well as students and

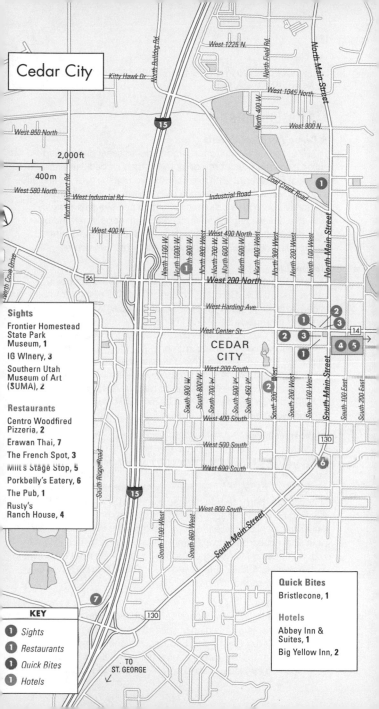

Cedar City

West 1225 N.

Kitty Hawk Dr.

North Bulldog Rd.

West 1045 North

North Field Rd.

North Main Street

West 900 N.

West 400 N.

Coal Creek Road

West 850 North

West 580 North

North Airport Rd.

West Industrial Rd.

Industrial Road

Industrial Road

West 400 N.

West 400 North

North 1100 West

North 1000 W.

North 900 W.

North 800 West

North 700 W.

North 600 W.

North 500 W.

North 400 West

North 300 West

North 200 West

North 100 West

West 200 North

West Harding Ave.

West Center St.

CEDAR CITY

West 200 South

South 900 W.

South 800 W.

South 700 W.

South 600 W.

South 500 W.

South 450 W.

West 400 South

South 300 West

South 200 West

South 100 West

South Main Street

South 100 East

South 200 East

West 500 South

West 600 South

South Ridge Road

West 800 South

South 1100 West

South 860 West

South Main Street

North Cove Drive

Sights

Frontier Homestead State Park Museum, **1**

IG Winery, **3**

Southern Utah Museum of Art (SUMA), **2**

Restaurants

Centro Woodfired Pizzeria, **2**

Erawan Thai, **7**

The French Spot, **3**

Milt's Stage Stop, **5**

Porkbelly's Eatery, **6**

The Pub, **1**

Rusty's Ranch House, **4**

Quick Bites

Bristlecone, **1**

Hotels

Abbey Inn & Suites, **1**

Big Yellow Inn, **2**

KEY

1 *Sights*

1 *Restaurants*

1 *Quick Bites*

1 *Hotels*

TO
ST. GEORGE

2,000 ft

400 m

faculty. ✉ *13 S. 300 W., Cedar City* ☎ *435/586–5432* ⊕ *www.suu. edu/suma* ⊘ *Closed Sun.*

🍴 Restaurants

★ Centro Woodfired Pizzeria

$ | PIZZA | You can watch your handmade artisanal pizza being pulled from the fires of the brick oven, then sit back and enjoy a seasonal pie layered with ingredients like house-made fennel sausage and wood-roasted cremini mushrooms. The creamy vanilla gelato layered with a balsamic reduction and sea salt is highly addictive. **Known for:** house-made sausage; good wine and beer list; creative desserts. ⑤ *Average main: $15* ✉ *50 W. Center St., Cedar City* ☎ *844/385–3285* ⊕ *www.centropizzeria.com.*

Erawan Thai

$ | THAI | In a nondescript but conveniently located shopping center just off the interstate, this excellent Thai restaurant has a cheerful, inviting, rustic-wood interior with paintings, crafts, and canisters of imported tea. The kitchen turns out deftly prepared renditions of classic dishes—chicken satay, *tom kha* soup—as well as such creative fare as mango-curry fried rice, barbecue chicken in Thai spices, and five different entrées featuring elk. **Known for:** attractive, art-filled space; crispy duck with several preparations; extensive selection of teas. ⑤ *Average main: $17* ✉ *1190 Sage Dr., Cedar City* ☎ *435/267–0391* ⊕ *www.facebook. com/erawanthaicedarcity* ⊘ *Closed Sun.*

★ The French Spot

$$ | FRENCH | This charming patisserie and bistro in the center of downtown is a favorite stop for lattes and cold brew; crepes and salads; heartier dinner specials (salmon, filet mignon, ratatouille); and ethereal pastries and sweets, including a rotating selection of chocolate, berry, lemon, and seasonal tarts. It's also perfect for stocking up on picnic supplies before a hiking or biking adventure. **Known for:** picnic supplies to enjoy before a show at the nearby Utah Shakespeare Festival; scrambled-egg breakfast croissants with ham, bacon, Gruyère, or smoked salmon; colorful macarons. ⑤ *Average main: $25* ✉ *18 S. Main St., Cedar City* ☎ *347/886–8587* ⊕ *www.thefrenchspotcafe.com.*

Milt's Stage Stop

$$$ | STEAKHOUSE | Cabin decor, friendly service, and canyon views are the hallmarks of this dinner spot 10 minutes southeast of downtown Cedar City by car. Expect traditional, hearty steak house cuisine: teriyaki beef kebabs, prime rib, and shrimp scampi, accompanied by loaded baked potatoes, deep-fried zucchini, and

Did You Know?

The Utah Shakespeare Festival (June through October), running since 1962, features performances of the Bard's works in an open-air replica of the Globe Theatre.

similar sides. **Known for:** scenic alpine setting; hefty steaks and seafood; apple crisp à la mode. $ *Average main: $32* ⌂ *3560 E. Hwy. 14, Cedar City* ☎ *435/586–9344* ⊕ *www.miltsstagestop.com* ⊙ *No lunch.*

The Pub

$ | CAFÉ | FAMILY | Don't be fooled by the name—coffee and tea are the only brews here. Build a sandwich of meat, egg, cheese, and more on a freshly baked bagel, croissant, artisan bread, or one of four flavors of wraps. **Known for:** walk from the Shakespeare Festival; espresso; seasonal soups. $ *Average main: $10* ⌂ *86 W. Center St., Cedar City* ☎ *435/867–1400* ⊕ *www.thepubcedarcity. com.*

Porkbelly's Eatery

$ | AMERICAN | As the name suggests, this airy contemporary restaurant is a meat-lover's paradise. Starting with tri-tip eggs Benedict and chicken and waffles at breakfast, pulled-pork sandwiches, carne asada nachos, and bacon-mushroom-cheddar burgers follow. **Known for:** mammoth portions of meat-centric fare; smoked baby back ribs on weekends; the chicken bomb (a jalapeño stuffed with cream cheese and sausage and wrapped in chicken and bacon). $ *Average main: $18* ⌂ *565 S. Main St.* ☎ *435/586–5285* ⊕ *www.porkbellyseatery.com* ⊙ *Closed Sun. and Mon.*

Rusty's Ranch House

$$ | STEAKHOUSE | Locals have long considered the meals at this fun, if a bit touristy, Old West–style roadhouse some of the best in the region. They serve steaks, barbecue brisket and baby back ribs, towering burgers, sweet coconut shrimp, and other classics. **Known for:** extensive cocktail selection; quirky Western vibe; Granny's hot-caramel apple cobbler. $ *Average main: $28* ⌂ *2275 E. Hwy. 14* ☎ *435/586–3839* ⊕ *www.rustysranchhouse.com* ⊙ *Closed Sun. No lunch.*

☕ Coffee and Quick Bites

Bristlecone

$ | CAFÉ | Drop by this airy, contemporary, downtown coffeehouse—which adjoins a yoga studio that offers a wide range of classes—for the best espresso drinks in town, including bourbon barrel–aged cold brew and crème brûlée cappuccinos. There's also an extensive menu of flavored lemonades and fresh-squeezed juices, plus tasty breakfast items like blackberry parfait and chai oatmeal. **Known for:** outstanding, locally roasted coffee beans; yoga and pilates classes; healthy breakfast fare and salads.

⑤ *Average main: $8* ⊠ *67 W. Center St.* ☎ *435/708–0000* ⊕ *www. bristleconeco.com.*

🛏 Hotels

Abbey Inn & Suites

$ | **MOTEL** | A few blocks from the interstate and near Southern Utah University, this two-story economical motel has spacious rooms with exterior entrances, refrigerators, microwaves, and—in the case of suites—kitchens and jetted tubs. **Pros:** centrally located; reasonable rates; nice indoor pool and fitness center. **Cons:** road noise for some rooms; bland setting amid fast-food restaurants and chains; cookie-cutter room decor. ⑤ *Rooms from: $139* ⊠ *940 W. 200 N, Cedar City* ☎ *435/586–9966, 800/325–5411* ⊕ *www.abbeyinncedar.com* ⬏ *83 rooms* ⦾ *Free Breakfast.*

★ Big Yellow Inn

$ | **B&B/INN** | Many of the rooms in this stately Georgian Revival inn are more reminiscent of Colonial Williamsburg than the Utah high desert, but they contain the kinds of plush amenities you'll appreciate if celebrating a special occasion or a grand theater weekend—think stone fireplaces, large balconies, and claw-foot tubs or Jacuzzis. **Pros:** elegant, rambling old home; in a pleasant, leafy residential neighborhood; a few minutes' walk to Shakespeare Festival and downtown dining. **Cons:** books up in advance during summer festival season; frilly, old-fashioned room decor; on a slightly busy street. ⑤ *Rooms from: $139* ⊠ *234 S. 300 W, Cedar City* ☎ *435/586–0960* ⊕ *www.bigyellowinn.com* ⬏ *12 rooms* ⦾ *Free Breakfast.*

🛍 Shopping

Bulloch's Drug

CANDY | **FAMILY** | Built in 1917 and remodeled to retain its historic character, this landmark building in downtown Cedar City contains an old-fashioned drug store, complete with a soda fountain from the 1950s. Enjoy ice cream, shakes, sundaes, and malts, or try one of the uniquely flavored sodas. And then pick up a few treats at the candy counter, or browse the adjacent gift shops, where you'll find a tempting selection of toys and souvenirs. ⊠ *91 N. Main St.* ☎ *435/586–9651* ⊕ *www.bullochdrug.com.*

★ Red Acre Farm CSA

OTHER FOOD & DRINK | **FAMILY** | Run by the engaging mother-daughter team of Symbria and Sara Patterson, this organic and biodynamic farm in a fertile valley 6 miles north of Cedar City is a wonderful side trip for visitors of all ages. The farmstand fashioned out of

recycled materials stocks seasonal fruits and veggies, plus eggs, cheese, baked goods, and jams. You can also learn about sustainable agriculture on a free farm tour (given twice monthly) and visit with the friendly goats, pig, dairy cow, and llama, and a two-bedroom suite in the farmhouse is available for overnight stays. ⊠ *2322 W. 4375 N* ☎ *435/865–6792* ⊕ *www.redacrefarmcsa.org.*

Tropic

12 miles southeast of Bryce Canyon City.

Just a few miles farther from the national park than Bryce Canyon City but considerably cuter, tiny Tropic (population 500) is a convenient base for exploring the region's majestic rock formations— many of which you can see from town. You'll find a handful of eateries and lodgings here, some of them excellent. Keep in mind that many businesses shut down or greatly slow down in winter.

GETTING HERE AND AROUND

Just down the hill from Bryce Canyon, tiny Tropic is along Highway 12.

🍽 Restaurants

★ i.d.k. Barbecue

$ | **BARBECUE** | **FAMILY** | This casually hip, counter-service restaurant with picnic tables outfitted with big rolls of paper towels serves tender pulled pork, smoked chicken, and beef brisket barbecue, along with classic sides like macaroni and cheese, baked beans, potato salad, and cornbread. You can enjoy your barbecue as a platter or sandwich, or take things to another level and try it smothered over nachos or in a loaded baked potato. **Known for:** nice variety of both sweet and spicy sauces; chalkboard menu with creative staff recommendations; peach cobbler. $ *Average main: $12* ⊠ *161 N. Main St., Tropic* ☎ *435/679–8353* ⊕ *www. idkbarbecue.com* ⊗ *Closed Sun.*

★ The Stone Hearth Grille

$$$ | **MODERN AMERICAN** | With sweeping panoramas toward Bryce Canyon from the back deck, an art-filled dining room with a stone fireplace, and some of the most accomplished modern American fare within an hour's drive of the park, this refined yet unpretentious restaurant on the outskirts of tiny Tropic is well worth a splurge. Favorites here include the salad of citrus-roasted carrots with avocado and coconut cream, the bone-in grilled pork chops with cheddar potato fondue, and several preparations of local grass-fed steaks. **Known for:** breathtaking views; great children's menu; well-curated wine list. $ *Average main: $36* ⊠ *1380 W. Stone Canyon La., Tropic* ☎ *435/679–8923* ⊕ *www.stonehearth-grille.com* ⊗ *Closed Nov.–Feb. No lunch.*

🛏 Hotels

Bryce Trails Bed & Breakfast

$ | **B&B/INN** | This contemporary B&B set in a sagebrush canyon just outside Tropic's small downtown offers a number of noteworthy perks, including a delicious made-from-scratch breakfast, close access to a trail that leads right into the park, and individually decorated rooms hung with the dazzling landscape photography of owner Edgars Erglis—one-on-one photography classes are offered, too. **Pros:** friendly hosts who know a lot about the area; superb, hearty breakfast included; within hiking distance of Bryce Canyon. **Cons:** not a good fit for children; two-night minimum during some busy periods; about a mile from downtown restaurants. $ *Rooms from: $164* ⊠ *1001 Bryce Way, Tropic* ☎ *435/231–4436* ⊕ *www.brycetrail.com* ⮑ *7 rooms* ❖ *Free Breakfast.*

Bybee's Steppingstone Motel

$ | **MOTEL** | This cheerfully decorated, economical, and intimate seven-unit boutique property in tiny downtown Tropic is just 15 minutes east of the park and on the way toward Escalante. **Pros:** individually decorated rooms; short walk from several restaurants; Keurig coffeemakers and tea kettles in rooms. **Cons:** check-in office has limited hours; pets not allowed; no breakfast (but oatmeal and granola bars are provided). ⑤ *Rooms from: $109* ✉ *21 S. Main St., Tropic* ☎ *435/574–9432* ⊕ *www.bybeesteppingstone. com* ⊘ *Closed Dec.–Mar.* ⇱ *7 rooms* ⦿ *No Meals.*

★ Stone Canyon Inn

$$ | **B&B/INN** | Although technically not in the park, this stunningly situated luxury inn lies just east of Bryce Canyon, and rooms and the excellent on-site restaurant, The Stone Hearth Grille, have astounding views of the park's hoodoos—there's even a trailhead nearby that accesses some of Bryce's best trails. **Pros:** the most luxurious rooms in the area; fantastic restaurant on site; soaking tubs and fireplaces in some rooms. **Cons:** sometimes books up far in advance; not within walking distance of downtown shops and restaurants; no breakfast. ⑤ *Rooms from: $207* ✉ *1380 W. Stone Canyon La., Tropic* ☎ *435/679–8611, 866/489–4680* ⊕ *www. stonecanyoninn.com* ⇱ *15 rooms* ⦿ *No Meals.*

Escalante

39 miles northeast of Tropic.

Though the Dominguez and Escalante expedition of 1776 came nowhere near this area, the town's name does honor the Spanish explorer. It was bestowed nearly a century later by a member of a survey party led by John Wesley Powell, charged with mapping this remote area. Today, this friendly little town is home to a growing crop of lodgings, eateries, and tour operators. Escalante is the northern gateway to Grand Staircase–Escalante National Monument, an amazing wilderness that earned monument status in 1996. It's also a popular base for visitors to both Bryce Canyon and Capitol Reef national parks, which it lies roughly midway between.

GETTING HERE AND AROUND

Escalante is accessible by Highway 12, one of the prettiest drives in the state, especially the stretch that runs north to Boulder. You can explore the vast Grand Staircase–Escalante National Monument via unpaved roads (some of which are pretty rough), ideally with a four-wheel-drive vehicle, although in dry weather, a

A surreal canyon in Grand Staircase–Escalante, a national monument administered by the Bureau of Land Management.

passenger car can handle some areas. Several key access points are off Highway 12. It costs nothing to enter the park, but fees apply for camping and backcountry permits.

◉ Sights

★ Calf Creek Recreation Area

NATURE SIGHT | FAMILY | One of the more easily accessible and rewarding adventures in the national monument, this picturesque canyon rife with oak trees, cacti, and sandstone pictographs is reached via the 6-mile round-trip Lower Calf Creek Falls Trail, which starts at Calf Creek Campground, 15 miles east of Escalante and 12 miles south of Boulder along scenic Highway 12. The big payoff, and it's especially pleasing on warm days, is a 126-foot spring-fed waterfall. The pool at the base is a beautiful spot for a swim or picnic. ⊠ *Hwy. 12* ☎ *435/826–5499* ⊕ *www.blm.gov/visit/calf-creek-recreation-area-day-use-site* ⛁ *$5 per vehicle.*

Escalante Petrified Forest State Park

STATE/PROVINCIAL PARK | FAMILY | This park just 2 miles northwest of downtown protects a huge repository of petrified wood, easily spotted along two short but moderately taxing hiking trails (the shorter and steeper of the two, the Sleeping Rainbows Trail, requires some scrambling over boulders). Of equal interest is the park's Wide Hollow Reservoir, which has a swimming beach and is popular for kayaking, stand-up paddleboarding, trout fishing, and birding. Keep an eye out for Escalante Rock Shop, just before

you reach the park border, which sells petrified wood and other geological wonders. ⊠ *710 N. Reservoir Rd.* ☎ *435/826–4466* ⊕ *stateparks.utah.gov/parks/escalante-petrified-forest/* ⊠ *$10 per vehicle.*

★ Grand Staircase–Escalante National Monument

NATIONAL PARK | This breathtaking, immense, and often difficult-to-access wilderness became a national monument in 1996. And although its federal status continues to generate controversy that has led to reductions and subsequent restorations of its boundaries, this nearly 1.9-million-acre tract of red rock canyons, stepped escarpments (the Grand Staircase), sheer rock ridges, and sweeping mesas continues to beguile hikers, canyoneers, and other outdoors enthusiasts. Unlike parks and monuments operated by the National Park Service, Grand Staircase–Escalante is administered by the Bureau of Land Management (BLM), and visiting its key attractions requires a bit more research and effort than, for example, Bryce or Capitol Reef, which are relatively more compact and accessible.

The best way to plan your adventures within the park is by stopping by one of the four visitor centers in the area, the best of these being the stunning Escalante Interagency Visitor Center in downtown Escalante. The smaller BLM Visitor Center in Cannonville is also helpful, or if you're entering the monument from the south, check out the BLM Visitor Centers in Kanab and Big Water. Given that many of the monument's top attractions are in remote areas with limited signage and access via unpaved (and sometimes very rough) roads, many visitors hire one of the area's many experienced outfitters and guides—this is an especially smart strategy if it's your first time in the area. Some of the monument's top attractions are big draws—including Calf Creek Recreation Area and the several hikes and vistas along Hole-in-the-Rock Road accessed from Escalante, the Burr Trail up near Boulder, and the Paria Movie Set and Paria Canyon–Vermilion Cliffs Wilderness east of Kanab. ⊠ *Escalante Interagency Visitor Center, 755 W. Main St.* ☎ *435/826–5499* ⊕ *www.blm.gov/programs/national-conservation-lands/utah/ grand-staircase-escalante-national-monument.*

Hell's Backbone Road

SCENIC DRIVE | For a scenic, topsy-turvy backcountry drive or a challenging mountain-bike ride, follow 35-mile Hell's Backbone Road (aka Forest Road 153) from Escalante, where it begins as Posey Lake Road, to Boulder. Built by the Civilian Conservation Corps in the early 1930s, it's a gravel-surface alternate route to scenic Highway 12. You can make the drive with an ordinary passenger car in summer (it's impassable in winter), assuming dry conditions, but a four-wheel-drive vehicle is more comfortable. Allow about two hours to drive it. At roughly the midway point, the dramatic 109-foot-long Hell's Backbone Bridge, which crosses over a breathtaking 1,500-foot chasm, makes for a memorable photo op. ⊠ *Hell's Backbone Rd.*

★ Highway 12 Scenic Byway

SCENIC DRIVE | Keep your camera handy and steering wheel steady along this entrancing 123-mile route that begins at U.S. 89 just south of Panguitch and meanders in a generally northeasterly direction through Red Canyon, the south end of Bryce Canyon National Park, and the towns of Escalante and Boulder, before climbing Boulder Mountain and winding through the Dixie National Forest to Torrey, just west of Capitol Reef National Park. The roughly 25-mile stretch from Escalante to Boulder is the most spectacular. Allow time to pull off and stop at the many scenic overlooks; almost every one will give you an eye-popping view, and interpretive signs let you know what you're looking at. Pay attention while driving, though. The road is sometimes twisting and steep—the section over Hogback Ridge, with its sheer dropoffs on both sides, will really get your heart pumping. ⊠ *Hwy. 12.*

Hole-in-the-Rock Road

SCENIC DRIVE | On the way to southeastern Utah in 1879, Mormon pioneers chipped and blasted a narrow passageway in solid rock, through which they lowered their wagons. The Hole-in-the-Rock Trail, now an extremely rugged 60-mile unpaved washboard road that's officially known as BLM 200, leads south from Highway 12, 5 miles southeast of Escalante, to the actual hole-in-the-rock site in Glen Canyon National Recreation Area. The original passageway ends where the canyon has been flooded by the waters of Lake Powell—you can hike the half-mile from the end of the road to a dramatic viewpoint overlooking the lake.

Just keep in mind that it can take up to three hours to drive to the end of the road, and high-clearance vehicles are best (and a requirement when muddy—check with the Escalante Interagency Visitor Center before setting out). However, there are some amazing hiking spots located along the route, including Zebra Slot Canyon (at mile 8.5) and Devil's Garden (at mile 12), which are less daunting to reach. Other worthwhile hikes and stops along the route include Peek-A-Boo Gulch (off Dry Fork Road, at mile 26) and Dance Hall Rock (at mile 36). ⊠ *Hole-in-the-Rock Rd.* ⊕ *www. nps.gov/glca/learn/historyculture/holeintherock.htm.*

★ Kodachrome Basin State Park

STATE/PROVINCIAL PARK | FAMILY | Yes, this remarkable landscape in Cannonville, about 40 miles southwest of Escalante, is named after the old-fashioned color photo film, and once you see it you'll understand why the National Geographic Society gave it the name. The stone spires known as "sand pipes" are found nowhere else in the world. Hike any of the trails to spot some of the 67 pipes in and around the park. The short Angel's Palace Trail takes you quickly into the park's interior, up, over, and around some of the badlands. Note that the oft-photographed Shakespeare Arch collapsed in 2019; although the trail leading to what is now a pile of rubble is still open, it's not as interesting as the Angel's Palace or Panorama Trails. ⊠ *Off Cottonwood Canyon Rd.* ✛ *9 miles southeast of Cannonville* ☎ *435/679–8562* ⊕ *stateparks. utah.gov/parks/kodachrome-basin* ⊠ *$10 per vehicle.*

🍴 Restaurants

★ Escalante Outfitters Restaurant

$ | AMERICAN | This warm and inviting log cabin–style restaurant—operated by a local tour operator that also runs a camp store and cabin and camping compound—is a great place to sit back and relax after a day of hiking, fly-fishing, or road-tripping. Try one of the creatively topped pizzas, a veggie sandwich, or an apple-pecan-arugula salad, or drop in for a well-crafted (Fair Trade) coffee and a light breakfast to kick off the day. **Known for:** excellent craft beer selection; friendly crowd; fine coffees, quiches, and pastries in the morning. ⑤ *Average main: $15* ⊠ *310 W. Main St., Escalante* ☎ *435/215–7953* ⊕ *www.escalanteoutfitters.com* ☉ *Closed Dec.–Feb.*

Georgie's Outdoor Mexican Cafe

$ | MEXICAN | FAMILY | This quirky food truck–style café beside Canyons of Escalante RV Park doles out filling and flavorful Mexican and Southwestern standbys, including prodigious chicken or beef burritos with Oaxacan and Jack cheese and house-made green salsa, and seasoned-cod tacos with aioli. There's ample seating on the cheerful patio. **Known for:** flan with weekly rotating flavors; lavender lemonade and other nonalcoholic drinks; colorfully painted outdoor seating area. ⑤ *Average main: $13* ⊠ *495 W. Main St., Escalante* ☎ *435/826–4782* ⊕ *www.facebook.com/georgiesoutdoormexicancafe* ☉ *Closed Sun. and Mon.*

Nemo's Drive-Thru

$ | BURGER | FAMILY | Dive into one of the hefty burgers at this local fast-food spot set in a low-slung mid-century building on Main Street—there's no indoor seating, just order at the counter and

The National Geographic Society gave colorful Kodachrome Basin State Park its very apt name.

enjoy your meal at one of the green picnic tables. Bison, beef, and veggie patties are available, along with beer-battered-cod baskets, corn dogs, pulled pork sandwiches, and homemade ice cream and shakes. **Known for:** pralines-and-cream milkshakes; mushroom and Swiss burgers; old-fashioned, family-friendly ambience. ⑤ *Average main: $11* ⌧ *40 E. Main St.* ☎ *435/826–4500* ⊕ *www. burgeralien.com* ⊙ *Closed Sun.*

🖥 Coffee and Quick Bites

★ Kiva Koffeehouse
$ | **CAFÉ** | This fun stop along scenic Highway 12, about 13 miles east of Escalante, was constructed by the late artist and inventor Bradshaw Bowman, who began building it when he was in his eighties and spent two years finding and transporting the 13 Douglas-fir logs surrounding the structure. The distinctive eatery with amazing views serves a daily-changing array of made-from-scratch soups, bagel sandwiches, tamales, oatmeal pancakes, salads, and decadent desserts, plus exceptional coffee and espresso drinks. **Known for:** breathtaking canyon views; creative, farm-to-table breakfast and lunch fare; sticky date pudding, apple crumb pie, and other treats. ⑤ *Average main: $10* ⌧ *Hwy. 12* ✛ *Between mileposts 73 and 74* ☎ *435/826–4550* ⊕ *www.kivakoffeehouse. com* ▭ *No credit cards* ⊙ *Closed Mon. and Tues. and Nov.–Feb. No dinner.*

Hotels

★ Entrada Escalante Lodge

$ | **B&B/INN** | Each of the eight rooms in this smart, contemporary lodge in downtown Escalante has a patio with grand views of the surrounding mountains, plus plenty of cushy perks like French presses and fresh-ground coffee, plush bedding, and 50-inch smart TVs. **Pros:** convenient downtown location; spacious rooms with Grand Staircase views; pets are welcome in some rooms. **Cons:** books up well ahead many weekends; in a very secluded, small town; great coffee but no breakfast. $ *Rooms from: $180* ✉ *480 W. Main St.* ☎ *435/826–4000* ⊕ *www.entradaescalante. com* ☾ *Closed Jan. and Feb.* ⇥ *8 rooms* ⊙ *No Meals.*

Escalante Outfitters Cabins

$ | **B&B/INN** | If you don't care about frills but do plan on adventuring in the area, consider one of this property's seven simple but cute log cabins, which share a bathhouse, or the large family cabin that sleeps four and has its own bathroom; tent sites are also available. **Pros:** firepit, grills, and picnic tables; pet-friendly; guided tours available on site. **Cons:** cabins are tiny; you may have to wait in line for a shower; some cabins have only bunk beds. $ *Rooms from: $55* ✉ *310 W. Main St.* ☎ *435/215–7953* ⊕ *www.escalanteoutfitters.com* ☾ *Closed Dec.–Feb.* ⇥ *8 cabins* ⊙ *No Meals.*

Escalante Yurts

$$ | **B&B/INN** | **FAMILY** | Sitting on a peaceful pinyon- and sagebrush-shaded mesa a couple of miles north of town, this mini glamping compound comprises seven warmly outfitted yurts, each with year-round climate control, top-of-the-line linens, a patio with gas grill, a well-stocked kitchen or kitchenette, and an ample sitting area with a TV. **Pros:** plenty of space between each yurt allows for lots of privacy; peaceful setting that's ideal for stargazing; four-wheel-drive Jeep rentals available on site. **Cons:** Wi-Fi can be a little slow; pets not allowed; not within walking distance of town. $ *Rooms from: $239* ✉ *1605 N. Pine Creek Rd.* ☎ *435/826–4222, 844/200–9878* ⊕ *www.escalanteyurts.com* ⇥ *7 yurts* ⊙ *Free Breakfast.*

★ Slot Canyons Inn

$ | **B&B/INN** | In a dramatic, New Mexico adobe–style building, this upscale inn with spacious rooms and lots of big windows is 5 miles west of town—at the mouth of a canyon on the edge of the national monument—and has hikes right outside its door, as well as hosts who are happy to provide guidance on regional treks. **Pros:** utterly peaceful, enchanting setting; within a short hike of petroglyphs and dramatic cliffs; many rooms have jetted soaking tubs. **Cons:** remote location; the cheapest room is a little small; not within walking distance of town. $ *Rooms from: $149* ✉ *3680 Hwy. 12* ☎ *435/826–4901* ⊕ *www.slotcanyonsinn.com* ⬐ *11 rooms* ¡○¡ *Free Breakfast.*

★ Yonder Escalante

$ | **RESORT** | **FAMILY** | Of the several hip glamping resorts that have opened in southern Utah in recent years, this sprawling compound on the west side of Escalante might just offer the best balance of a gorgeous contemporary design—accommodations are in sleekly restored Airstream trailers and cozy glass-walled cabins—and a welcoming communal spirit, thanks to an inviting patio served by a food truck, a huge pool, and a drive-in movie theater with seating in vintage autos. **Pros:** fun common spaces that are perfect for making new friends; lots of thoughtful amenities; expansive view of the high desert and mountains. **Cons:** social atmosphere isn't for everyone; no private bathrooms in many units (but the common bathhouses are gorgeously appointed); not within walking distance of town. $ *Rooms from: $189* ✉ *2020 W. Hwy. 12* ☎ *435/274–7222* ⊕ *www.stayyonder. com* ⬐ *40 units* ¡○¡ *No Meals.*

Nightlife

★ 4th West Pub

BARS | In a part of the world where nightlife typically consists of listening to coyotes howl beneath a starlit sky, it's nice to have one good late-night ("late" meaning 10 or 11 pm, depending on the season) option. The stylishly converted, circa-1940s service station is a great place to socialize, shoot pool, and sip craft beer and cocktails. There's live music, art classes, trivia matches, and other fun events on some evenings, and the kitchen turns out tasty bar snacks, from nachos to panini. ✉ *425 W. Main St.* ☎ *435/826–4525* ⊕ *www.4wpub.com.*

🛍 Shopping

★ Escalante Mercantile & Natural Grocery

FOOD | Although ostensibly a grocery store—and one with an excellent selection of organic produce, fine cheeses, baked goods, prepared foods to go, and other gourmet items—this friendly market in a historic brick house also features a coffeehouse and smoothie café with patio seating and a small gallery with well-curated art, crafts, and gifts. ✉ *210 W. Main St.* ☎ *435/826–4114* ⊕ *www.facebook.com/escalantemerc.*

⚡ Activities

ADVENTURE TOURS
Excursions of Escalante
LOCAL SPORTS | Hiking, backpacking, photography, and canyoneering tours in the Escalante region are custom-fit to your needs and abilities by experienced guides. Canyoneers have the chance to explore slot canyons, moving through slot chutes and rappelling down walls and other obstacles. All gear and provisions are provided whether it's a day hike or multiday adventure. ⊠ *125 E. Main St.* ☎ *800/839–7567, 435/826–4714* ⊕ *www.excursionsofescalante.com* 🎟 *From $165*.

HIKING
Escape Goats
HIKING & WALKING | **FAMILY** | This noted family-owned outfit offers a variety of day and evening hikes, multiday backpacking trips, and photo and artist tours, which can be customized to any ability or age. Half- and full-day "herbal" tours acquaint participants with the medicinal and healing qualities of flora that grows naturally in Grand Staircase–Escalante. The company provides shuttle services, too. ☎ *435/826–4652* ⊕ *www.escalantecanyonguides.com* 🎟 *From $150*.

★ Utah Canyon Outdoors
HIKING & WALKING | Run by a young husband and wife team with extensive experience in Utah as naturalists and guides, this stellar outfitter operates an outdoor gear shop and coffeehouse in a charming little converted house in downtown Escalante. In addition to full-day hikes through slot canyons and the area's other dramatic features, the company also offers Escalante yoga experiences. ⊠ *325 W. Main St.* ☎ *435/826–4967* ⊕ *www.utahcanyonoutdoors.com* 🎟 *From $150*.

Index

Photo Credits

Front Cover: RGB Ventures/SuperStock/Alamy Stock Photo [Descr.:Hikers are seen in Zion Narrows section Virgin River in Zion National Park Utah]. **Back cover, from left to right:** Arkanto/Shutterstock. Oleksii Gavryliuk/Shutterstock. Lu_sea/Shutterstock. **Spine:** Josemaria Toscano/Shutterstock. **Interior, from left to right:** My Good Images/Shutterstock (1). Pixelshop/Shutterstock (2-3). **Chapter 1: Experience Zion and Bryce Canyon National Parks:** Checubus/Shutterstock (6-7). Wisanu Boonrawd/Shutterstock (8-9). Moehlestephen/Dreamstime (9). Anastassiya Bornstein/Shutterstock (9). Greater Zion Convention & Tourism Office (10). Matt Morgan/Visit Utah (10). Brester Irina/Shutterstock (10). Mark Bolen/Shutterstock (10). Prajit Ravindran/Visit Utah (11). Atmosphere1/Shutterstock (11). Cheri Alguire/Shutterstock (11). Greater Zion Convention & Tourism Office (11). Steve Greenwood/Visit Utah (12). Barbara Ash/Shutterstock (12). Margaret.Wiktor/Shutterstock (12). Subway Zion/Visit Utah (13). Harry Collins Photography/Shutterstock (16). Nina B/Shutterstock (16). MichaelJust/iStockphoto (16). James_Gabbert/iStockphoto (16). AGAMIstock/iStockphoto (17). Mosslight Fine Art Photography/iStockphoto (18). Allison Herreid/Shutterstock (19). Karel Triska/Shutterstock (20). Trekandshoot/Dreamstime (20). Courtesy of VisitUtah/iStockphoto (20). Jay Dash Photography/Courtesy of Visit Utah (20). Hpbfotos/Dreamstime (21). Courtesy of Visit Utah (21). Matthewtrain/Dreamstime (21). Courtesy of Garfield County Office of Tourism (21). **Chapter 2: Travel Smart:** Gestalt Imagery/Shutterstock (44). **Chapter 3: Zion National Park:** Simon Dannhauer/Shutterstock (45). Bjul/Shutterstock (52). Sloot/iStockphoto (59). LouieLea/Shutterstock (61). Lu_sea/Shutterstock (62-63). Michael Andrew Just/Shutterstock (66). VivL/Shutterstock (68). Harry Beugelink/Shutterstock (74). Harry Beugelink/Shutterstock (82). **Chapter 4: Zion Gateways:** MelaniWright/Shutterstock (85). Gestalt Imagery/Shutterstock (92). Gestalt Imagery/Shutterstock (96). CheriAlguire/Dreamstime (105). Sumikophoto/Shutterstock (112**). Chapter 5: Bryce Canyon National Park:** Bpperry/Dreamstime (117). Paul Brady Photography/Shutterstock (131). Malfootu/Shutterstock (135). Dibrova/Shutterstock (138-139). Bill45/Shutterstock (141). Unai Huizi Photography/Shutterstock (142). Jaahnlieb/Dreamstime (144-145). Yingna Cai/Shutterstock (149). **Chapter 6: Bryce Canyon Gateways:** Bluejayphoto/iStockphoto (153). Oscity/Dreamstime (160). Wirepec/Dreamstime (164). Courtesy of Utah Shakespeare Festival (169). Galyna Andrushko/Shutterstock (175). Kojihirano/iStockphoto (176-177).Tashka/Dreamstime (181). **About Our Writer:** Photo is courtesy of the writer.

*Every effort has been made to trace the copyright holders, and we apologize in advance for any accidental errors. We would be happy to apply the corrections in the following edition of this publication.

Fodor's InFocus ZION AND BRYCE CANYON NATIONAL PARKS

Publisher: Stephen Horowitz, *General Manager*

Editorial: Douglas Stallings, *Editorial Director;* Jill Fergus, Amanda Sadlowski, *Senior Editors;* Brian Eschrich, Alexis Kelly, *Editors;* Angelique Kennedy-Chavannes, *Assistant Editor;* Yoojin Shin, *Associate Editor*

Design: Tina Malaney, *Director of Design and Production;* Jessica Gonzalez, *Senior Designer;* Jaimee Shaye, *Graphic Design Associate*

Production: Jennifer DePrima, *Editorial Production Manager;* Elyse Rozelle, *Senior Production Editor;* Monica White, *Production Editor*

Maps: Rebecca Baer, *Senior Map Editor;* Mark Stroud (Moon Street Cartography), *Cartographer*

Photography: Viviane Teles, *Director of Photography;* Namrata Aggarwal, Neha Gupta, Payal Gupta, Ashok Kumar, *Photo Editors;* Jade Rodgers, *Photo Production Intern*

Business and Operations: Chuck Hoover, *Chief Marketing Officer;* Robert Ames, *Group General Manager*

Public Relations and Marketing: Joe Ewaskiw, *Senior Director of Communications and Public Relations*

Fodors.com: Jeremy Tarr, *Editorial Director;* Rachael Levitt, *Managing Editor*

Technology: Jon Atkinson, *Executive Director of Technology;* Rudresh Teotia, *Associate Director of Technology;* Alison Lieu, *Project Manager*

Writer: Andrew Collins

Editor: Jacinta O'Halloran

Production Editor: Elyse Rozelle

3rd Edition

ISBN 1346 309X

ISSN 978-1-64097-672-6

All details in this book are based on information supplied to us at press time. Always confirm information when it matters, especially if you're making a detour to visit a specific place. Fodor's expressly disclaims any liability, loss, or risk, personal or otherwise, that is incurred as a consequence of the use of any of the contents of this book.

SPECIAL SALES

This book is available at special discounts for bulk purchases for sales promotions or premiums. For more information, e-mail SpecialMarkets@fodors.com.

PRINTED IN CANADA

10 9 8 7 6 5 4 3 2 1

About Our Writer

 Former Fodor's staff editor **Andrew Collins** is based in Mexico City but spends a good bit of the year traveling throughout the United States, and the Four Corners region in particular. A longtime contributor to more than 200 Fodor's guidebooks, including *National Parks of the West*, *Utah*, *Santa Fe*, *Pacific Northwest*, *Inside Mexico City*, and *New England*, he's also a regular contributor to The Points Guy travel webiste. He's written for dozens of mainstream and LGBTQ publications—*Travel + Leisure*, *New Mexico Magazine*, *AAA Living*, and *The Advocate* among them. Additionally, Collins teaches travel writing and food writing for New York City's Gotham Writers Workshop. You can find more of his work at ⊕ *AndrewsTraveling.com*, and follow him on on Instagram @TravelAndrew.

Fodor's Travel

Give us your feedback on this book!
Take a quick survey at fodors.com/survey and get a free
digital copy of *10 Great Walks in Our Favorite Cities*.

Where to next?
...e our complete list on fodors.com/guidebooks

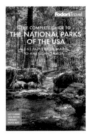

Fodor's has guides covering more than 7,500 destinations!
Available in bookstores and online.

Visit Fodors.com

⊘ Trip ideas and inspiration

⊘ Tips and recommendations

⊘ Connect with fellow travelers
fodors.com/community

⊘ Subscribe to our newsletter
fodors.com/newsletter/signup

f 🐦 𝓟 📷 @FODORSTRAVEL

Fodor's InFocus
ZION & BRYCE CANYON NATIONAL PARK

Ready to Go Away?

The experts at **Fodor's** are here to help. We're bringing you the very best of **Zion and Bryce Canyon National Parks**, including **rim trails**, **canyon treks**, **the Narrows**, and more. Our local experts vet every recommendation to ensure that you have all the essential information to plan a perfect trip and make the most of your time.

Get Inspired

- **Ultimate experience guide** to the top things to see and
- **Full-color photo features** to spark your wanderlust
- **Everything you need to know** before you go

Get Planning

- **Convenient itineraries** to maximize your time
- **Practical tips** that go beyond the standard advice
- **Detailed maps** to help you navigate confidently

Get Going

- **Unmissable sights** from hanging gardens to hoodoos
- **Hotels and restaurants** expertly selected for every taste
- **Insider advice** on where to find under-the-radar gems

"Fodor's is pitched a few notches higher...aimed at a fairly discerning traveler with an appetite for background and the occasional surprise." –**NEW YORK TIMES**

3RD EDITION

ISBN 978-1-64097-672-6

5 1 4 9 9

9 781640 976726

US $14.99

FODORS.COM
Find the latest travel news and inspiration and connect with other travelers in our forums.